Simply Chopin

Simply Chopin

WILLIAM SMIALEK

SIMPLY CHARLY
NEW YORK

Copyright © 2018 by William Smialek

Cover Illustration by José Ramos
Cover Design by Scarlett Rugers

All rights reserved. No part of this publication may be reproduced, distributed, or transmitted in any form or by any means, including photocopying, recording, or other electronic or mechanical methods, without the prior written permission of the publisher, except in the case of brief quotations embodied in critical reviews and certain other noncommercial uses permitted by copyright law. For permission requests, write to the publisher at the address below.

permissions@simplycharly.com

ISBN: 978-1-943657-18-6

Brought to you by http://simplycharly.com

Contents

Other *Great Lives*	vii
Preface	viii
Series Editor's Foreword	xi
Portrait of Frédéric Chopin at 25	xii
1. Early Years	1
2. Education and Coming of Age 1825-1830	6
3. Exit from Warsaw 1831-1838	22
4. Chopin and Sand 1839-1847	39
5. Illness and Final Years 1848	52
6. Chopin's Legacy	55
Sources	59
Suggested Reading	62
About the Author	64
A Word from the Publisher	65

Other *Great Lives*

Simply Austen by Joan Klingel Ray
Simply Beckett by Katherine Weiss
Simply Beethoven by Leon Plantinga
Simply Chekhov by Carol Apollonio
Simply Chomsky by Raphael Salkie
Simply Darwin by Michael Ruse
Simply Descartes by Kurt Smith
Simply Dickens by Paul Schlicke
Simply Dirac by Helge Kragh
Simply Einstein by Jimena Canales
Simply Eliot by Joseph Maddrey
Simply Euler by Robert E. Bradley
Simply Faulkner by Philip Weinstein
Simply Fitzgerald by Kim Moreland
Simply Freud by Stephen Frosh
Simply Gödel by Richard Tieszen
Simply Hegel by Robert L. Wicks
Simply Hitchcock by David Sterritt
Simply Joyce by Margot Norris
Simply Machiavelli by Robert Fredona
Simply Napoleon by J. David Markham & Matthew Zarzeczny
Simply Nietzsche by Peter Kail
Simply Proust by Jack Jordan
Simply Riemann by Jeremy Gray
Simply Sartre by David Detmer
Simply Tolstoy by Donna Tussing Orwin
Simply Stravinsky by Pieter van den Toorn
Simply Turing by Michael Olinick
Simply Wagner by Thomas S. Grey
Simply Wittgenstein by James C. Klagge

Preface

In Jerzy Andrzejewski's 1948 novel *Ashes and Diamonds* (Popiół i diament), centered on the conflicting political factions in Poland at the end of World War II, a celebratory banquet ends with the inebriated guests dancing the stately polonaise (this word means the musical piece has Polish origins) at the urging of the hotel impresario.

> Kotowicz [hotel impresario] was proposing something to the musicians in a secretive whisper. They eyed each other, undecided. Kotowicz drew back and looked at them as if to judge the effect of his words.
> "Well? Gentlemen!"
> The young pianist who had remained in the background until now came over to his colleagues. "What does he want us to play?"
> "Chopin's Polonaise."
> "Which one?"
> "Heaven knows! How can we play it?"
> The pianist went up to Kotowicz.
> "Which polonaise do you want us to play?"
> The other eyed him contemptuously.
> "In A flat, young man, A flat."

The film based on this book, also called *Ashes and Diamonds* (1958), was directed by the celebrated Polish director Andrzej Wajda. The movie captures the scene which follows that exchange as the ending to a boisterous party, with an ad hoc group of drunken musicians stumbling through a polonaise as they accompany the pianist on their diverse instruments.

The scene draws on one of Frédéric Chopin's best-known compositions, a well-recognized symbol of Poland, partitioned and occupied as it was during the composer's lifetime

(1810–1849). Instilled with national elements and hope for independence through the choice of musical material reflecting the homeland, Chopin's works continue to permeate the Polish ethos and artfully project it to the world through performance and scholarship.

In another vein, his structural intricacies have ensured a prominent place for the composer in the 19th-century Romantic era. His works attracted the consideration of music theorist Heinrich Schenker as he formulated a new process of analyzing the harmonic structure of selected musical compositions. Schenkerian analysis graphs the underlying structure of a musical work, isolating the harmonic progression supporting the layers of melodic detail that initially reaches our ears. Graphic distillations of Chopin's music prepared by Schenker, along with the works of other 19th-century composers, provided new insight into the compositional process. Musical analysis has uncovered the changing complexity of tonal relations presented in Chopin's developing musical style.

A Polish composer and pianist whose artistic creations exhibited the expressive strengths of his instrument and drew upon the folk idiom of his homeland, Chopin acquired a multi-dimensional role in history. In the opinion of the late American pianist Charles Rosen, "there is an urbane, worldly aspect to Chopin's style that partly accounts for his immense popularity; it has also given him a bad name among amateurs who take their music earnestly." In any case, Chopin had a profound influence on keyboard music.

With virtuosic fast passages and sentimental melodic phrases, his compositions are often characterized as "salon music," suitable to be played in front of small groups of people gathered in private homes. But as the references to literary works, film, and musical analysis reveal, Chopin's life and works have left us with a multifaceted legacy of his importance to 19th-century music. Research over the past several decades has provided new perspectives on the facts of his life as related to his correspondence, publishing activities, national orientation, performance style, and even health.

The manuscript sequence of Chopin's masterworks is available on the Internet for open study. The taxonomy of his published music in different countries has been traced as well. Many of his works have been analyzed individually, and changes in musical style over his artistic oeuvre carefully considered. Chopin's many letters provide insight into his relationships, values, and activities, and these can be related to his creative works. The sesquicentennial of his death in 1999 and the bicentennial of his birth in 2010 were full of concerts and scholarly conferences that displayed new views of this composer's place in history. *Simply Chopin* may be a misleading title for this accessible portrait of one of the most intriguing figures in music history.

William Smialek
Tyler, Texas

Series Editor's Foreword

Simply Charly's "Great Lives" series offers brief but authoritative introductions to the world's most influential people—scientists, artists, writers, economists, and other historical figures whose contributions have had a meaningful and enduring impact on our society.

Each book provides an illuminating look at the works, ideas, personal lives, and the legacies these individuals left behind, also shedding light on the thought processes, specific events, and experiences that led these remarkable people to their groundbreaking discoveries or other achievements. Additionally, every volume explores various challenges they had to face and overcome to make history in their respective fields, as well as the little-known character traits, quirks, strengths, and frailties, myths, and controversies that sometimes surrounded these personalities.

Our authors are prominent scholars and other top experts who have dedicated their careers to exploring each facet of their subjects' work and personal lives.

Unlike many other works that are merely descriptions of the major milestones in a person's life, the "Great Lives" series goes above and beyond the standard format and content. It brings substance, depth, and clarity to the sometimes-complex lives and works of history's most powerful and influential people.

We hope that by exploring this series, readers will not only gain new knowledge and understanding of what drove these geniuses, but also find inspiration for their own lives. Isn't this what a great book is supposed to do?

Charles Carlini, Simply Charly
New York City

Portrait of Fryderyk Chopin at 25 by Maria Wodzińska.

1. Early Years

Chopin's life and musical career began in Poland, a provincial region well east of the major cities—Paris, Vienna, London, and Berlin among them—that were becoming the epicenter of European cultural life in the 19th century.

Fryderyk Franciszek Chopin was born into a modest family in Żelazowa Wola, on March 1, 1810. There is frequently confusion about his birthdate because his baptismal certificate indicates February 22, 1810, as the date of his birth. At present, the village of Żelazowa Wola hosts a museum dedicated to the early years of the composer's life, and is a popular tourist attraction.

Chopin's parents were Tekla Justyna Krzyżanowska (1782-1861) and Nicolas Chopin (1771-1844), who from 1802 was employed by Countess Ludwika Skarbek at Żelazowa Wola to tutor her children. Nicolas, a native of Lorraine, had migrated from France during the Napoleonic Period to make his life as a teacher in the Polish territory, and Frédéric's French family background integrated with his Polish upbringing accompanied the composer throughout his life. Frédéric had three sisters, Ludwika, Justyna Izabella, and Emilia. In the family's middle-class household, music was an intrinsic part of parents and children's life, influencing young Frédéric's musical development from the earliest age.

In the 19th century, the idea of Poland was an abstraction, linking a noble past with a hopeful future. With the completion of a third partition by Russia, Prussia, and Austria in 1795, Poland was eliminated from the political map of Europe.

Although Napoleon's 1806 reorganization of Central Europe had created a separate state identified as the Duchy of Warsaw, the country was divided again into three parts among the same nations, and this division remained in place throughout the 19th century and into the first decades of the 20th. The defeat of Napoleon and the subsequent treaty signed at the Council of Vienna in 1815 established the Polish Kingdom under a modern and liberal constitution, but the country did not achieve independence; it was ruled by the Russian Czar Alexander I's brother, Grand Duke Constantine. As the source of Enlightenment ideals, France was a natural partner to the Poles, explaining Nicolas Chopin's journey eastward.

In October of Chopin's birth year, the family moved to Warsaw when Nicolas began working for the Warsaw Lyceum. In 1812, he accepted a position as a French lecturer at the Szkoła Artylerii i Inżynierii (School of Artillery and Engineering) in Warsaw, and two years later, he became a lecturer in French literature and language at the Warsaw Lyceum. In 1820, he was named professor of French at the Szkoła Wojskowa Aplikacyjna (Army Apprentices College).

The family's move provided young Frédéric with great opportunities for his musical development. As a provincial capital and center of Polish culture, this city of over 100,000 inhabitants in the 1820s, offered exposure to musical events, as concerts transitioned from aristocratic country manors to public venues. Newspapers of the period document the sponsorship of musical presentations and the many performers who traveled to Warsaw to concertize. Music clubs and associations provided additional settings for the growing cultural scene in the city. At the same time, aristocratic circles offered private venues for exhibiting musical talent, especially of a developing young artist such as Chopin.

Frédéric began piano lessons at the age of six with Wojciech Żywny (1756-1842), a Czech immigrant. He continued to teach Chopin from 1816 to 1822. According to Wojciech Sowiński, an early Chopin biographer, Żywny was a disciple of Bach, who instructed Chopin in the German classical method used in Poland at that time. The focus of this early preparation was learning piano works of Bach and Mozart, as was later evident in Chopin's stylistic development as a composer. Study of Bach's works, providing a thorough understanding of counterpoint, was common among composers of Chopin's generation. Frédéric's sister Ludwika also studied piano, and the two children often played duets with four hands.

The cultivation of Chopin's gifts as a composer of piano music began in the next year when he was 7. Although his early works, simple variations and marches, are lost, his first composition, the *Polonaise in B-flat major* notated by his father, shows early promise. Chopin's *Polonaise in G minor*, dedicated to Wiktoria Skarbek, Countess Ludwika's cousin, was published by J.J. Cybulski in 1817. Izydor Józef Cybulski was a music engraver in Warsaw who managed his own printing workshop from 1805-1817. A review of this polonaise in a prominent Warsaw periodical describes the boy as "a true musical genius." The work reflects Chopin's knowledge of works by earlier Polish composers, such as Karol Kurpiński and Michał Kleofas Ogiński, and is similar to other polonaises turned to dance pieces designed for the salon. In his biographical sketch of Chopin, Sowiński wrote that the worship of Chopin for Poland was painted in his music; the nuances were rendered in his polonaises, mazurkas, and ballades.

The geopolitical changes in the Polish territories supported a growing national culture around Warsaw. Publications such as *Śpiewy historyczne* (Historical Songs, 1816) by Julian Ursyn Niemcewicz stimulated a Polish awareness, which would become a theme of Chopin's creative work. The earlier generation of Polish composers who contributed music to this volume—Karol Kurpiński, Franciszek Lessel, and Maria Szymanowska—created a musical environment in Warsaw that could nurture the development of emerging artists outside of aristocratic country estates, as was the norm in prior decades. In his public debut on February 24, 1818, Chopin performed the *Concerto in E minor* by Vojtech Jirovec at a soirée of the Towarzystwo Dobroczynności (Charitable Society) at the Radziwiłł palace, which once belonged to a Polish noble family but in 1817 became the seat of the Tsarist Governor.

The next October, Nicolas had the boy present a gift of two Polish dances to Tsarina Maria Teodorovna, the Tsar's mother. Over the following year, Frédéric performed in the salons of numerous Polish aristocrats, as well as at the Belvedere Palace, which, at that time, was the residence of Russian Grand Duke Constantine. A frequent guest of the Grand Duke, Chopin dedicated a march to him. This initiative could only help the family attract sponsorship for the young boy. Chopin was dedicated to him, as a part of the family's solicitation of sponsors for the young boy.

During this period, while Nicolas Chopin taught French, the family lived on the Warsaw University campus in an apartment on Krakowskie Przedmieście that can be identified now through a historical marker on the building. Childhood friends, including Jan Białobłocki and Jan Matuszyński, would become lifelong correspondents, whose epistolary exchanges with the composer have provided considerable insight into his personal life and artistic development. Chopin continued his musical studies with Wojciech Żywny and dedicated the *Polonaise in A-flat major* to this teacher. In 1822, he began his studies with the most prominent Warsaw musician of the period, Józef Elsner (1769-1854). Of German descent, Elsner settled in Warsaw in 1799, where he was active as a composer, conductor, and pedagogue. Under his direction, the Conservatory, known as the Instytut Muzyki i Deklamacji (Institute of Music and Declamation), opened on April 25, 1821.

Beginning with private composition lessons in 1822, Chopin later continued his studies with Elsner at the Instytut Muzyki. In conjunction with his growing activity as a composer, Chopin was emerging as a keyboard performer in Warsaw. He performed a concerto by Ferdinand Ries at a benefit concert for the Towarzystwo Dobroczynności in February 1823, with other concerto performances later that spring. In September, Chopin started his formal secondary school education and entered the fourth grade of the Warsaw Lyceum.

Frédéric spent the summer of 1824 in north-central Poland, in the village of Szafarnia on the estate of a family friend. During this time, the young composer socialized with the local nobility and listened to Polish folk music in the neighboring villages. Until this point, the reflection of Polish traditions in Chopin's music was isolated in the early composition of polonaises, an aristocratic Polish dance. However, the exposure to village life and Polish folklore associated with the life cycle of family celebrations extended Chopin's sensitivity to Polish traditions in his music and can be found specifically in the composition of mazurkas and the infusion of folk-influenced melodies in his piano works. It was also in Szafarnia that the playful aspect of his personality emerged with the writing of the "Kurier Szafarski," a newsletter of local news that he sent to his parents in Warsaw.

Returning to the capital after the summer to complete his secondary education, Chopin continued his musical activities. He experimented in performing on newly invented instruments, such as the eolomelodicon and aeolopantaleon, and was engaged as a church organist. Throughout this period, he also continued composing music and promoted the broader awareness of his creative musical ideas by publishing the *Rondo in C minor*, op. 1 with the firm of Antoni Brzezina, a music publisher who owned a bookshop in Warsaw from 1822 to 1825. The composition achieved notice in the Leipzig musical journal *Allgemeine Musikalische Zeitung*.

The next year, when he was 15, Frédéric entered the Conservatory.

2. Education and Coming of Age 1825-1830

Frédéric's studies at the Lyceum ended in 1827, leaving him free to concentrate on his musical ambitions. Enrollment at the Szkoła Główna Muzyki (Main School of Music), or Warsaw Conservatory, initiated the period of Chopin's formal education in music. This institution, founded in 1823, was connected to Warsaw University and directed by Józef Elsner. The university itself was founded in 1816 for students who were, for the most part, the sons of the landed gentry and prosperous burghers.

In a very real sense, entry to the Conservatory was simply a continuation of Chopin's individual work with Elsner; however, the institution's educational resources and study along with other talented students also contributed to his development as a composer. Although Chopin was not destined to remain in Warsaw for his musical career, the opportunities presented to him until his permanent departure from Poland in 1830 have left us with early works of significance. It is clear from these compositions, created under the auspices of structured musical education, that his sense of the classical style was well-formed, but that he was also allowed to explore his own creative approaches to form and tonal structure.

The political realities of life in Warsaw were changing. The Congress Kingdom of Poland, placed under the control of Russia at the Congress of Vienna, lasted only 15 years. As King of Poland, Russian Tsar Alexander I (ruled 1801-1825), had granted the country a constitution which called for an elected legislative body, wide suffrage (by the standards of the day), the retention of the Napoleonic civil code, freedom of the press and religion, and exclusive use of the Polish language. Nevertheless, from the beginning of the Congress Kingdom, the Tsar and his government paid little attention to this constitution authorizing Polish self-government, and when Nicholas I (ruled 1825-1855) became Russian Tsar and Polish King after Alexander's death, he began openly to trample upon constitutional rights, intensifying political oppression through police reprisals. The Polish gentry originally believed he could be controlled through the Sejm, the Polish parliament, but they later realized that this was fruitless.

Cultural conditions in Warsaw were formed out of Poland's political history. At the time, Polish musical life was centered in Warsaw, with the many limitations of music-making having an impact on Chopin's education. The young composer became well known to the local aristocrats who attended his salon concerts. Piano performances were central to Warsaw's salons and musical compositions based on national elements, such as the polonaise, were popular. Although it was not common for someone of Chopin's middle-class background to attend salon gatherings among aristocrats, he developed the social manners and bearing to be accepted in that circle. Warsaw's salon gatherings were similar to those in other European cities; however, topics of discussion tended to relate more to politics and national concerns than to social and cultural issues of the day. During his Warsaw period, Chopin became active in various types of salons, including those hosted by aristocrats, literati, and Warsaw University faculty.

We can see that the young composer was nurtured in his youth by both the public and private sides of Warsaw's musical life. Although he had an independent audience of aristocrats and nobility, he also was affected by the conditions of public musical events in the city, such as the absence of a permanent orchestra. In the 18th century, there had been many active orchestras in Poland, serving both aristocratic courts and monasteries. The early history of the Polish symphony is in this way connected to church music, as evidenced by the number of extant symphonic manuscripts found in monastery collections. But with the gradual shrinking of the country as a political unit by partition and the consequent difficulties of court life, financial resources were not available to maintain large instrumental ensembles and other cultural luxuries. As much of the nobility moved to the major cities, the urban population greatly increased. Between 1800 and 1825, Warsaw's population doubled. City life did provide for the establishment of new cultural institutions but, unfortunately, a permanent orchestra was not among them; the Filharmonia Narodowa (National Philharmonic) was founded in 1901. However, opera was popular in Warsaw, and the characteristics of early Polish opera required only a small orchestra.

Chopin's involvement in church music during his formative years underscores the significance of churches in Warsaw's musical life in the 1820s. Chamber music was widely performed, and instrumentalists could be organized into a larger orchestra for an occasional concert, such as the performances of Chopin's concertos, although it should be noted that the rehearsals and performances of the concertos were frequently accompanied by chamber groups.

The travels of the prodigious composer

In the summer of 1826, Frédéric traveled to Duszniki, a prominent spa town southeast of Warsaw in Silesia. Physicians had prescribed the curative waters at this spa for his sister Emilia, so Chopin traveled there with his mother and two sisters. The improvement of his own health was a bonus because throughout his life he was characterized by his family as possessing a less than vigorous constitution. Daily walks were a fitting aspect of the wellness and social activities of the stay in Duszniki. While there, Frédéric gave two charity concerts benefiting orphaned children. Later that summer, he spent time in the village of Strzyżewo, on the estate of his godmother Anna Emilia Wiesiołowska (1793-1873), and attended musical performances where he met local musicians who had a strong impact on his musical development. After attending a performance of Rossini's comic opera *La Gazza ladra*, he used one of the themes in the trio of the *Polonaise in B-flat minor*. It was at this time that he first met Prince Antoni Radziwiłł (1775-1833) at the Prince's nearby estate. Antonin. Radziwiłł pursued his own amateur artistic interests as a musician and composer. His best known musical work is an opera on the theme of *Faust* (the protagonist of a classic German legend). Time in the countryside provided Frédéric with exposure to Polish folk and national music, as well as the inspiration to adopt some of its characteristics—particularly the rhythms of folk dances and melodic scale patterns—into his own compositions.

Back in Warsaw, Chopin's musical education continued. Situated behind the university were a number of educational facilities for the training of musicians, including the Instytut Muzyki i Deklamacji (Institute of Music and Declamation), also known as the Warsaw Conservatory. In 1826, this institution was subdivided into the Szkoła Główna Muzyki, which remained attached to Warsaw University, and the Szkoła Dramatyczna i Śpiewu (School of Drama and Singing). Other young composers studying at the school at this time included Ignacy Feliks Dobrzyński (1807-1867), Julian Fontana (1810-1869), Tomasz Napoleon Nidecki (1807-1852), Józef Nowakowski (1800-1865), and Edouard Wolff (1816-1880). School friends from these early years, as evidenced by their voluminous correspondence, provided support for the composer throughout his life.

As his career progressed, Chopin started to suffer from a respiratory condition that would limit his activities in the future. On April 10, 1827, his younger sister, the 14-year-old Emilia, died of tuberculosis. Despite this disruption in his personal life at a time when he was absorbed in his musical studies, Frédéric passed his final exam in composition and earned Elsner's notation that he had "szczególna zdolność" (special talent). This praise incited Brzezina and Co., a Warsaw publishing house of the period, to publish the *Rondo in C minor* as Op.1 in 1825, when Chopin was only 15 years old. This rondo, structured in the traditional form with a repeated theme alternating with contrasting sections, was created as a piano showpiece. Similar to Chopin's other early works, the composition stems from his ease with improvisation and virtuoso display at the keyboard. His early (1827) composition titled *Variations on 'La ci darem la mano'*, op. 2, was dedicated to his childhood friend Tytus Wojciechowski (1808-1879).

After exams at the end of the 1826-27 academic year, Frédéric spent the summer months in Gdańsk, a city on the Baltic coast. While traveling, he once again experienced the music of the Polish countryside at social gatherings. Before the start of the next academic year, the Chopin family moved to the Krasiński Palace on the opposite side of Warsaw's main thoroughfare, Krakowskie Przedmieście. In this new residence, the family hosted musical salons on Thursdays and invited local musicians and poets who would later inspire Frédéric's musical compositions. Although some of the works from this period are lost, we still have two *Waltzes in A-flat Major*, a *Mazurka in A minor* (WN13), and the initial work on the song "Precz z moich oczu" ("Disappear from my sight"), a setting of a poem by the national poet Adam Mickiewicz (1798-1855).

During the winter of 1827-28, Chopin composed his *Sonata in C minor*, Op. 4 dedicated to Elsner. Clearly schooled in the works of master composers of the past—Bach and Mozart among them—his musical expression in a traditional genre, such as the sonata, was obviously inspired by Elsner's teaching. Early in Frédéric's creative life, this was an important contribution to his development. He did not compose many works in this traditional form, but the concept of thematic development and tonal contrast so infused in the sonata tradition can be sensed in all his piano compositions. On July 22, 1828, he passed the final exam in composition with Elsner's evaluation about his "amazing talent" and a note that he needs to take a leave to "improve his health."

Creative work in traditional musical forms continued over his summer vacation outside of Warsaw at Strzyżewo, most notably with the *Trio*, Op. 8, completed the following spring. At the end of the summer of 1828, Chopin traveled to Berlin to attend concerts and opera performances. Among the opera performances he attended were those of Gaspare Spontini, *Ferdinand Cortez* (1809); Domenico Cimarosa, *Il Matrimonio segreto* (1792); George Onslow, *Le Colporteur* (1827); and Carl Maria von Weber, *Der Freischütz* (1821). Frederick Niecks, an early biographer, explained that Chopin was accompanied on this trip by Dr. Feliks Jarocki, a professor at Warsaw University and colleague of Chopin's father, who was invited to a congress in Berlin. The visit spanned the weeks of September 9-28, 1828. In addition to attending excellent performances, Chopin visited the music shop of music publisher Adolf Martin Schlesinger–Schlesinger'sche Buchhandlung–to become acquainted with the newest musical publications. Visiting Poznań on the return trip, Chopin gave a concert there on October 2, playing Haydn, Beethoven, and Hummel in the palace of Prince Antoni Radziwiłł, Duke Governor of the Grand Duchy of Posen. Upon returning to Warsaw four days later, Chopin participated in local cultural activities by playing a two-piano version of the *Rondo in C Major*, Op. 13 (1828) with Julian Fontana (1810-1865). By the end of December, he completed the *Rondo à la Krakowiak*, Op. 14. (Krakowiak, so named after the city of Krakow, is a fast dance in duple meter.

Like Chopin's other early works, this piano piece begins with a slow introduction and continues in the spirit of improvisation before settling into the krakowiak rhythm of the title. Other works from this period include a set of three *Polonaises*, Op. 71 and three *Ecossaises*, Op. 72.

Since Warsaw had its cultural limitations, visiting major cities of Europe became part of the educational experience for young Polish people. As the century progressed, increasing numbers of Polish artists and writers studied first in Berlin, but also in Vienna and Dresden. Whether in a university setting, or through private instruction with a well-known teacher, these foreign tours enabled the students to immerse themselves in the mainstream of European culture–to perform, attend concerts, and meet local artists as a means of expanding their experience outside of the isolation of the eastern lands. Several of Frédéric's friends from his youth also migrated to Paris in later years.

Chopin's correspondence documents how important his foreign experience was in establishing a viable musical career through publishing, but the letters also reveal his hesitation at performing in public concerts. His most intimate correspondents were also friends from this early period, especially Titus Wojciechowski and Jan Matuszyński.

In this period of Chopin's creative life, his music is often referred to as his "brillante style"–spirited, highly ornamented, and virtuosic. The foundation of these works is virtuoso technique and keyboard passagework that is improvisatory. The *Rondo* Op. 1, which draws on a krakowiak rhythm, fits this characterization, as does the Op. 2 *Variations on the Mozart melody from the opera Don Giovanni*, "La Ci darem la mano." Chopin's rendition of this popular melody is structured with a long introduction incorporating hints of the well-known melody, then the theme, and six variations, followed by a bravura finale. These early works were well suited to the public concerts given by Chopin in Warsaw.

At the core of Chopin's oeuvre over the course of his life were short piano pieces built on Polish rhythms. The krakowiak and mazurka are Polish folk dances; the polonaise, also infused with Polish sentiment, is an aristocratic dance. The framework of Polish dances provides a three-part form as a structural foundation. Piano pieces in these genres were composed by other Polish musicians, such as Ignacy Feliks Dobrzyński (1807-1867), and Józef Nowakowski (1800-1865), yet it was Chopin's creativity that took these stylized dance pieces from a condensed formal mold to expanded compositions.

In April 1829, the 19-year-old Chopin became infatuated with Konstancja Gładowska (1810-1889), an accomplished singer and emerging local talent. His correspondence documents this developing relationship through the spring of that year and beyond. The spring of that year presented the rare opportunity in Warsaw to attend performances of the virtuoso violinists Niccolò Paganini

(1782-1840) and Karol Lipiński (1790-1861). Their violin technique and mastery were discussed in the musical press by Warsaw's critics, and likely influenced the piano technique displayed in Chopin's music. The *Variations in A major* (WN16), composed at this time, is possibly an example of this influence.

On July 20, the Szkoła Główna Muzyki held its graduation. In this third year of Chopin's formal musical education, Elsner wrote the evaluation that noted his pupil's "amazing capabilities, musical genius." With the completion of his formal musical training in 1829, the young composer deserved another trip abroad to enhance his education and exposure to current trends and musical styles. In mid-July, he departed for Vienna with friends, traveling through Opoczno, Miechów, and Kraków. A visit to the Jagiellonian University Library on July 23 was part of his sightseeing agenda in Kraków, which also included visits to the iconic Wawel Castle and the salt mines in Wieliczka. These same sites continue to be popular tourist attractions to this day. Resuming his travel through Biesko, Cieszyn, and Moravia, he arrived in Vienna on July 31.

Developing his skills in Vienna

At that time, Vienna maintained a high musical standing due to the prominence of Haydn and Beethoven. The Gesellschaft für Musikfreunde (Music Friends' Society), founded in 1814, served a changing and less aristocratic audience in the concerts it sponsored. By the late 1820s, music publishing and instrument manufacture emerged to foster a new public musical culture that was more middle class. Italian opera remained popular, along with concerts by virtuosos such as Paganini, choral events, and salon evenings.

Upon arrival in Vienna, Chopin immediately absorbed himself in the musical life of this cultural capital, guided by his former teacher Vàclav Vilém Würfel (1790-1832). Würfel knew the Chopin family and often worked with young Frédéric. He had left Warsaw in 1824 for Prague, and then Vienna from 1824 to 1826. Chopin attended concerts, a series of operas by prominent composers of the period, and with introductory letters from Elsner, met several composers. Composers of the first half of the 19th century who may be considered secondary in historical importance today would have been celebrated musicians at the time. Among these are Ignaz Moscheles (1794-1870), Heinrich Herz (1803-1888), and Frédéric Kalkbrenner (1785-1849). An important task during this journey abroad was a meeting with Tobias Haslinger. Elsner, his committed teacher and mentor, had sent the *Variations on "La Ci darem la mano"* and the first *Sonata* to the music publisher Tobias Haslinger, as an introduction of his young student to Viennese music circles with the intention of launching Chopin's career. In a letter to his family, Frédéric reported on his meeting: "[Haslinger] wants me to play in public. They tell me here that it would be a great loss for Vienna if I were to leave without being heard. All this is incomprehensible for me" (August 12, 1829). The following month, he wrote to his friend Tytus Wojciechowski, explaining that: "Haslinger, my publisher, told me it would be better for my compositions if I gave concerts in Vienna; that no one knows my name, that the compositions are difficult and recondite." (September 12, 1829). Chopin's deep reluctance to perform in large venues intensified throughout his years abroad.

Beyond the musical experiences, there were social invitations to aristocratic homes and salons. Only a month after his arrival, on August 11 and 18, Chopin gave concerts, at Austrian composer Count Gallenberg's request, at the Kärntnerthortheater. The programs included the *Variations*, Op. 2, to stimulate sales of his publications, and piano improvisations. The Viennese audience recognized Chopin as someone fresh and new, with a differentiated national sound. The German-language musical press—Zeitschrift für Kunst, Allgemeine Musikalische Zeitung, and Wiener Theater Zeitung—reported the success of these performances. Chopin considered this reception in planning his future. Writing to Tytus Wojciechowski in October 1829, Chopin related that

> Hube, who came back last week, after visiting Trieste and Venice, brought me some cuttings from the Viennese periodical Zeitschrift für Litteratur, in which my playing and compositions are discussed at length and highly praised,–forgive me for telling you this,–at the end they speak of me as a "Selbstkräftiger Virtuoz," and also as richly endowed by nature;... If you want to know what I intend to do with myself this winter, learn that I shall not stay in Warsaw; but where circumstances will lead me, I don't know. (October 3, 1829)

By August 19, it was time to move to Prague, where he attended a concert on August 22. Through letters of introduction, he met with local musicians, although there was no public performance in Prague. In a private performance in Toeplitz, he exhibited his skill at improvising on popular opera themes and Polish melodies. His reliance on Polish sounds in his piano performances contributed to the attention he attracted while touring. Throughout his travels, he met with Polish compatriots living abroad. In Dresden in late August and early September, he continued the expansion of his cultural experiences by attending local musical performances. By September 12, after traveling through Wrocław, he was back in Warsaw.

It was in this, his last period of Warsaw residence, that Chopin began composition of some of his best-known works. This was a productive time for him. The *Piano Concerto in F minor* was inspired by the first of his three lifetime romances, his infatuation with Konstancja Gładowska, a student at the Conservatory. She served as his muse. Other important compositions started during this period include the collections of études. A return visit to the Poznań area and the estates of his godmother, Anna Emilia Wiesiołowska, and Prince Antonin Radziwiłł was planned for the end of October through November 1829. He composed the *Introduction and Polonaise*, Op. 3 for cello and piano for the Prince. While working on the *Concerto in F minor*, Op. 21 he was monitoring reports of his Viennese performances as reviews were translated from German and printed in the Polish press. By the end of his visit to Antonin, he had notated several of the Études of the Op. 10 collection.

The composition of the Op. 10 and Op. 25 Études spanned seven years, beginning while Chopin was still living in Warsaw. In the opinion of pianist Charles Rosen, Chopin was the true inventor of the concert étude, at least in the sense of being the first to give it complete artistic form—a form in which musical substance and technical difficulty coincide. The composition of études, short didactic pieces, was common among pianist-composers of the period. According to Jim Samson, Emeritus Professor of Music at the University of London, the Op. 10 Studies have special importance in Chopin's output. More than any other works at this time, they acted as a bridge between the *brilliante* style of the apprentice years and the unmistakable voice of his maturity. Each piece exposes the performer to one technical problem and issue with finger technique. Opus 10 leans back to the *Preludes* of Johann Sebastian Bach, irrespective of the format, and it is the quality of the music that is an important achievement of the collection.

Returning to Warsaw from Vienna Chopin participated in a musical soirée at the Resursa Kupiecka, an active musical venue of the period, performing his *Variations*, Op. 2. The Resursa Kupiecka or Merchant's Club, organized in 1805, was a social organization committed to the maintenance and encouragement of Polish cultural identity. Musicians were prominent members of this club from the beginning, and this was the site for the performance of an early version of Chopin's *Concerto in F minor* on December 10, 1829. Choral music was presented in local churches. The city's main concert venue and opera stage was the Teatr Narodowy (National Theater). He also participated in the weekly meeting at the home of German composer Joseph Christoph Kessler. His calendar of musical activities continued into the new year. The *Concerto in F minor*, along with the *Grand Fantasy in A Major*, were first heard in private salons and with small instrumental groups as the orchestral accompaniment. On March 17, 1830, these pieces were presented for the first time in their final form at the Teatr Narodowy, accompanied by an orchestra conducted by Karol Kurpiński. Typical of concert programs of the period, other pieces were interspersed among the movements in this cycle. A second performance of the concerto was scheduled for March 22. While audience reception at the initial performance did not match Chopin's expectations, the audience responded more enthusiastically at the second concert.

> After my concerts there was a flood of press notices, particularly in the Polish Courier; though their praises were somewhat exaggerated, they were still possible. The Official Bulletin also devoted some pages to panegyrics, but with the best intentions, it included in one number such preposterous remarks that I felt desperate when I read an answer in the Polish Gazette, which quite justly deprived me of the exaggerated attributes given me by the other. You must know that in that article the Official Bulletin declared that the Poles should be as proud of me as the Germans are of Mozart; obvious nonsense. (April 10, 1830)

The two piano concertos and the Sonata Op. 4 are all based on the musical form that was traditional for such works. In its basic concept, the first movement of sonata form, or sonata-allegro form, presents an initial theme followed by a contrasting theme in a related key. The melodies are developed with a variety of compositional techniques through a succession of keys. The tension of the modulating keys is resolved when the initial themes are reintroduced in the original or tonic key. Although this formal scheme can be traced back to earlier models structured in two large divisions, by the 19th century, the theorist Adolph Bernard Marx described sonata form in three parts: an exposition of two principal themes, development of this melodic material, and recapitulation or restatement of the original themes. Most important is the resolution of the tonal change introduced with the second theme of the exposition. Interestingly, Chopin deviated from the tonal schemes that had become common in works based on the sonata principle. As University of California musicologist Anatole Leikin noted: "In some sonatas the tonal relationship in the exposition and recapitulation are openly reversed. Chopin's Op. 4, his *Trio* Op. 8, and the *E Minor Concerto* are famous examples of this reversal of Classical procedure. The first piano sonata, composed while Chopin was a student at the Szkoła Główna Muzyki and dedicated to Elsner, is monothematic, with the theme recapitulated in B minor and then in G minor.

Chopin's early travels sparked his desire to leave Warsaw for Vienna or Berlin, but also throughout that spring, he continued his romantic interest in Gładowska. He originally intended to leave Warsaw in the winter of 1829-30, and then postponed the trip until the summer of 1830. By May 1830, he had decided to travel to Vienna rather than Berlin, even though at the time he was actively working on the *Piano Concerto in E minor*. In his letter to Tytus Wojciechowski of May 15, 1830, Chopin discussed his work on this piano-orchestral composition. The impressionistic description of his intentions in composing the music provides some insight into his approach to composition.

> The Adagio of the new concerto is in E major. It is not meant to be loud, it's more of a romance, quiet, melancholy; it should give the impression of gazing tenderly at a place which brings to the mind a thousand dear memories. It is a sort of meditation in beautiful spring weather, but by moonlight. (May 15, 1830)

The *Variations*, Op. 2 was published by Haslinger at this time and was presented publicly at the National Theater on July 8 in a benefit concert for the singer Barbara Majerowa. Later that month, on July 24, Chopin attended, in the same venue, Gładowska's operatic debut. Agreeing with others and writing to his friend Tytus Wojciechowski, he believed that "there won't be a second Gładowska, as regards purity and intonation and higher emotions, as they are understood on the stage." (August 31, 1830)

Rehearsals of his music began to cause some stress, as colleagues were traveling and music for his fall tour was still underprepared. He wrote to the same friend:

> What shall I do? I leave here the 10th of next month, but I must rehearse my Concerto first, as the Rondo is finished. Kaczyński and Bielawski come to me tomorrow. My Polonaise with the Violoncello, and Trio, are to be rehearsed incognito at 10 in the morning, before Elsner, Ernemann, Żywny and Linowski. We shall play till we drop. (August 21, 1830)

After the summer, Chopin wrote 10 songs to poems from Stefan Witwicki's *Piosnki Sielskie*. As he related to Tytus, the tension of leaving Warsaw was building up to the point that his pen was forecasting his future:

> I think I shall go away to forget my home forever; I think I shall go away to die; and how dismal it must be to die anywhere else except where one has lived! How horrible it will be to see beside my death-bed some cold-blooded doctor or servant instead of my own family. (September 4, 1830)

By this time, the *Concerto in E minor* was heard in home rehearsals with a small chamber ensemble. Chopin noted:

> Last Wednesday I rehearsed my Concerto with the quartet. I was pleased, but not altogether; people say the finale is the best part of it, because it is the most comprehensible. (18 September 1830)

By the end of the month, on September 22, the *Concerto in E minor* was in rehearsal with an orchestra. Chopin's manuscripts reveal many mistakes that required editing throughout his creative life. The consequence would have a profound impact on the rehearsal of a new work with instrumentalists. On October 5 Chopin reported:

"After the orchestral rehearsal of the second Concerto, it was decided to give it in public ..."

(The work received outstanding critical reviews on the performance of October 11, including the comments of the key musical leaders of the period. "Kurpiński spoke of its originality, Elsner of its rhythm." (October 5, 1830)

Regarding the piano concertos, the orchestration has been criticized as relatively weak. It has even been speculated that Chopin had help from his fellow students Dobrzyński and Nidecki in scoring the works. Nevertheless, little attention in this judgment is given to the orchestral resources that may have been available in Warsaw during this period. It has been related that the concertos were often rehearsed and performed with string quartet accompaniment, a concession to opportunities for performance in this provincial capital. Study of the scores to the two Chopin piano concertos will reveal that only a bass trombone is scored in the works, as opposed to a full complement of three trombones. That other orchestral works of the period have the same instrumentation suggests a broader context for the scoring of these works.

The two piano concertos are among Chopin's best known and often performed compositions. They are also among the small number of Chopin's piano works with orchestral accompaniment. Ironically, these pieces, which continue to be popular with both performers and audiences, date from his early period in Warsaw, and in that regard, do not exhibit the full extent of his creative capacity.

The concertos confirm Chopin's unorthodox view of the relationship between tonality and formal design in sonata movements of the Warsaw years. The works exhibit a relaxation of dominant-tonic polarity expected in the conventional tonal scheme for a concerto of the period. The works have been shown to be modeled on concertos by Hummel and otherwise reflect compositional techniques of the period. For example, the first movement of the Op. 11 concerto presents the second subject in the dominant minor, and Chopin reversed the tonal relationships in the exposition and recapitulation from the conventional scheme. The finale of both concertos is based on Polish folk rhythms; Op. 11 on the krakowiak and Op. 21 on a mazurka rhythm.

In the decade of the 1820s, Warsaw was under considerable political distress. Polish cultural life was allowed to develop under Russian rule of the Congress Kingdom of Poland. But with the accession of Nicholas I to the Russian throne in 1825, a more repressive regime was in place. This ultimately led to the insurrection launched on November 29, 1830, by cadets of the Warsaw Military College. Suppressed by the Russian authorities in September 1831, the insurrection led to a time of even greater repression of Polish culture. As a result, numerous Polish artists and intellectuals emigrated to other European cities. When Chopin left Warsaw on November 20, 1830, he was never to return to Poland again.

3. Exit from Warsaw 1831-1838

As a political entity, the Polish lands have had a long history of changing geography stemming from a topology that allowed for conquering forces to claim ownership. Throughout Chopin's early years, it was Russian control of the territory, including the city of Warsaw, which provided the political and cultural background for his acceptance as an artist in noble and aristocratic circles.

In anticipation of the changing political climate, Chopin left Warsaw in 1830 to seek his musical fortune in the cities to the West. Ultimately, the political realities of his Polish home caused him to remain an expatriate, one of many intellectuals and artists who monitored events in their Polish homeland from residences in major European cities.

His farewell concert on October 11, 1830, at the National Theater, was well received by the public. It featured Chopin's *E Minor Concerto*, Op. 11 and *Grand Fantasy on Polish Airs*, Op. 13. Konstancja Gładowska sang arias in the second half of the concert, much to Chopin's satisfaction. Although he was ready to leave Warsaw shortly after the performance, his departure was postponed until November 2. During this time, the composer continued his creative works and finished the C major and A minor études for the Op. 10 collection. Hasty completion of these works could explain mistakes in the score, even though the need for corrections was becoming a characteristic of his working process. As Chopin left Warsaw for what was to be the final time, Conservatory students gave a farewell performance in his honor of Józef Elsner's *Zrodzony w polskiej krainie* (Born in the Polish Land) at the entrance to the city in Wola. His travels took him through Kalisz, where he met with Tytus Wojciechowski, and the two journeyed together through Wrocław, Dresden, Prague, and Vienna, attending musical performances along the way and relying on letters of introduction to meet prominent musicians in each city.

Writing from Wrocław about his musical activities there, Chopin related his experience with the local Resursa. "They give three such concerts a week. I found the orchestra, small, as usual, assembled for rehearsal, a piano and, as umpire, some amateur, named Hellwig, who is preparing to play the Moscheles E *flat major concerto*." Joseph Schnabel, the Kapellmeister, asked Chopin to try the piano. After hearing a few variations, "Schnabel was immoderately pleased, began begging me to play in the evening. Schnabel especially pressed me so earnestly that I could not refuse the old man. He is a great friend of Elsner; but I told him I am doing it only for him, as I have not played for some weeks. I have no desire to distinguish myself in Wrocław." (November 9, 1830)

From Dresden, where he arrived on November 12, Chopin reported attending a dinner with the city's Polish community, and then called on local musical supporters, visited Polish social circles, and attended opera performances and concerts. Upon arrival in Vienna on November 23, he lived at various inns, staying in the city for eight months. The impressive growth of his performance technique and musicianship since his earlier visit to Vienna in 1829 was evident to many in the music community. Chopin wanted to play some concerts in Vienna and then travel on to Italy, but the plan was abandoned due to revolutionary activity there. From Vienna, Chopin wrote to Jan Matuszyński: "You know what is happening to me, how glad I am that I am in Vienna, that I am making so many interesting and useful acquaintances, that I may be going to fall in love." (November 22, 1830). He immediately engaged in a familiar pattern of activities—attending concerts, meeting local musicians, and socializing with Polish families.

Yet, due to a variety of circumstances, Chopin had trouble attracting interest in a concert; consequently, his financial resources ran short. The November Uprising against Russian rule started in Poland on November 29, and the Viennese awareness of the Polish revolution influenced public interest in Chopin during his stay in Vienna. Along with Chopin's other artist compatriots, Wojciechowski returned to join the insurgents to Russian rule.

Writing to Elsner on January 26, 1831, Chopin indicated his anxiety over news of the November Insurrection and his duty to assume the role of a cosmopolitan artist.

It could be expected that the young composer, away from family and homeland, would be homesick over the Christmas holidays. Nevertheless, over the course of the winter of 1830-31, he composed the *Mazurkas*, Opp. 6 and 7, the *Nocturnes*, Op. 9, and several of the *Études*, Op. 10. By April he was sketching the *Scherzo in B minor*, Op. 20, *Ballade in G minor*, Op. 23, *Mazurkas*, Op. 17, and *Polonaise*, Op. 26. When attending musical salons, he was often asked to perform and improvise. On June 11, he performed the *E Minor Concerto* with an orchestra and continued composing through the remainder of his stay in Vienna, which ended on July 20.

The time in Vienna stimulated Chopin's creativity. The collections of Mazurkas Op. 6 and Op. 7 are based on a typical folkloric rhythm. Drone accompaniment patterns, taken from folk sources, are also evident. A characteristic of Polish folk music found in Chopin's works is the melodic use of an augmented fourth associated with the Lydian mode. The sound of this scale is replicated in playing from F to F on the white keys of the piano. All but two of the mazurkas in the Opp. 6-7 were composed during his eight months in Vienna. They are marked by the emergence of an increasingly well defined, highly personal music style. These works are fashioned in consistently regular and symmetrical musical phrase groups, forming an ABA structure. The Op. 7 collection exhibits greater embellishment of melodies, while the left hand maintains the triple meter rhythm with the melodic profile emphasizing the second beat of the measure, characteristic of the mazurka. Several of the works in these two sets begin with introductory statements. Remarkably for Chopin, each of the collections ends with a notably short piece. This will stand as just one of the unexplained turns in Chopin's compositional trajectory. Chromatically ornamented melodic lines are a feature in this change from his earliest musical style.

The *Nocturnes*, Op. 9 were also composed during the verdant creative period in Vienna. They reveal the influence of John Field, an earlier champion of the genre. Chopin's pieces characteristically spin, continuously unfolding lines in long phrases. Some have a contrasting middle section moving toward more development in the later examples of this genre. Repetitive arpeggios in the left-hand counter the melodic filigree of the upper sounding parts, often sounding like improvised variation. The *Nocturnes*, Op. 15, composed about the same time, present contrasting middle sections to the three-part form. (Nocturnes are mood pieces with lyric melodic lines.) The F major nocturne moves with a repeated rhythm in the left hand, steadily accompanying the melodic invention of the right hand. In the second nocturne, odd note groupings infuse a taste of the rubato tempo fluctuations that have become a part of Chopin performances. Chopin scholar Jeffrey Kallberg noted the musical changes with the *Nocturne in G minor*, Op. 15, no. 3. The work presents a simpler accompaniment pattern with rhythmic stress on the second beat, and the melody lacks the ornamentation of earlier nocturnes. There are elements of the mazurka and a religious chorale section. He proposed a context for these mixed characteristics, explaining the unusual features of the work to be a reflection of Polish Romantic nationalism.

    The Opus 10 collection of piano études requires a pianistic focus on the independence of the hands. Arpeggio patterns travel up and down the keyboard, and sections of contrary motion provide another means of sounding the entire keyboard. Melodic motion can be in an upper part or migrate to inner voices in the texture. Chromatic filigree might be exchanged for a homorhythmic texture, bringing the opposition of the hands together. Chopin was successful in mastering this piano technique with difficult fingering patterns, all through a concert-quality musical piece.

    Chopin's journey to Paris took him through Linz, Salzburg, Munich, and Stuttgart, although his passport had him traveling through Paris to London. And this may have been his original plan. In Munich, he performed the *Concerto in E minor* and *Grand Fantasy on Polish Airs* in a matinee concert. We should note that the piano concerti were composed in reverse order of their numbering by opus. It was the newer work, the Op. 11, that Chopin played most often during this period. Writing in Vienna, Chopin reflected:

> Everything I have seen abroad till now seems to me old and hateful, and just makes me sigh for home, for those blessed moments I didn't know how to value. What used to seem great today seems common; what I used to think common is now incomparable, too great, too high. The people here are not my people; they're kind, but kind from habit; they do everything too respectable, flatly, moderately. I don't want even to think of moderation. (Spring 1831)

He was in Stuttgart when he learned the news of the fall of the November Uprising and the capture of Warsaw on September 8, 1831. In the document known as the Stuttgart Diary, Chopin made notes expressing his distress about the fall of the insurrection. This news of his homeland, as Chopin traveled abroad, instigated deeply felt emotions about family and friends at home, as well as the future of the Polish nation.

> Father! Mother! Where are you? Corpses? Perhaps some Russian has played tricks–oh wait–wait–But tears–they have not flowed for so long–oh, so long, so long I could not weep–how glad–how wretched–Glad and wretched–If I'm wretched I can't be glad–and yet it is sweet–This is a strange state–but that is so with a corpse; it's well and not well with it at the same moment. (Stuttgart, after September 8, 1831)

The impact of this upheaval inflected the musical expression in the next period of his life.

On Christmas Day in 1831, he wrote to Wojciechowski, indicating his critical view of the presentation of Polish music:

> You know how I have longed to feel our national music, and to some extent have succeeded in feeling it;–sometimes [Sowinski] gets hold of something of mine, now here, now there; something the beauty of which often depends on the

accompaniment; and starts to play it in a tipsy, cackling, pothouse or parish organ style; and there's nothing you can say, because he won't understand anything beyond what he has picked up.

In Paris, Poles and Polishness had risen in popularity because of the insurrection. Chopin was attracted to Paris as a city that would support the further development of his musical career. Yet, all have not agreed on the benefits of Parisian culture for the advancement of his emerging career.

> "Paris, this capital of the arts, guide of young talent, a city that dazzles the eyes of its victims, an enchanting stay for some, a consuming pit for others, the city where all the artists bring their inspirations, their dreams of glory, and their hopes. Paris was not conducive to the early beginnings of Chopin."

Arriving in Paris, he rented a furnished apartment on 27 Boulevard Poissonière. He arrived there with very few introductions, but in a short time he met prominent musicians; some, like Frédéric Kalkbrenner (1785-1849), held Chopin in the highest regard. Renowned as a touring virtuoso, Kalkbrenner was a strong proponent of his teaching method concentrating on independent development of the fingers. Chopin played the E *Minor Concerto* and other works for him, but ultimately chose not to study with Kalkbrenner; these lessons required a three-year commitment, including an assessment of the student's ability and adoption of Kalkbrenner's style. Elsner agreed with Chopin's reluctance to accept this plan.

Musicianship and social connections went hand in hand. Writing to Dominik Dziewznowski, Chopin intimated about his social life and its relationship to working:

> I have got into the highest society; I sit with ambassadors, princes, ministers; and even don't know how it came about,

Exit from Warsaw 1831-1838 | 27

because I did not try for it. It is a most necessary thing for me, because good taste is supposed to depend on it. At once you have a bigger talent if you have been heard at the English or Austrian embassy . . . I have five lessons to give today; you think I am making a fortune? Carriages and white gloves cost more, and without them one would not be in good taste. (1832)

As earlier, Chopin began attending musical performances, maintaining his familiarity with the latest trends. He was attracted to literary romanticism and art, and the emerging style of grand opera. He commented on concerts and opera performances in his voluminous correspondence. Writing to Józef Elsner in Warsaw, he reflected: "To be a great composer, one must have enormous knowledge, which, as you have taught me, demands not only listening to the work of others, but still more listening to one's own." (December 14, 1831)

He composed the first ballade and first scherzo, both expanding the sonata structure, during these early years in Paris. The changes with these works in a new genre reflect Chopin's role in the growth of Romanticism in music. The first *Ballade*, Op. 23, exhibits the tonal ambiguity that would increasingly become part of Chopin's music. As an extended work, the music begins outside of the main key, related to the waves of tension and release that follow. Interestingly, this ballade incorporates waltz elements. In Viennese music culture, the waltz represents a dance rhythm outside of the traditional Polish dances in other compositions. Chopin's first work in the genre, the Op. 23, became the ballade most popular with 19th-century audiences and critics. Like several of the later ballades, the balance in the work leans toward the end, much different than in traditional sonata-based works.

The *Polonaise* Op. 26 moves away from the standard dance toward expressing even greater affirmation of Polish identity. As a reaction to the 1830 Insurrection and its aftermath, this is consistent with other shifts stimulated by the political situation. Artistic response depended on whether one stood within the Polish borders, since internal censorship limited overt expressions of patriotism.

It was in Paris on November 17, 1831, that Chopin first met Countess Delfina Potocka, who would become a lifelong friend. She was a singer and, after 1832, his piano student. In 1945, Potocka's great-granddaughter, Paulina Czernicka, publically disclosed unknown letters from Delfina to Chopin suggesting they had an affair. Forensic research ultimately proved the letters to be fake, but the issue was long argued in the Chopin literature.

Composing, performing, and publishing

Also soon after moving to Paris, he expanded his publishing activities with several music publishers. A collaboration with cellist Auguste Franchômme (1808-1884), one of the first musicians he met in the city, inspired the publication of the *Polonaise in C major*, Op. 3, and composition of the *Grand Duo Concertante*, Op. 16A, based on a theme from the opera *Robert le diable*.

By this time, the distinguished composer Robert Schumann had reviewed the *Variations*, Op. 2 in the Allgemeine Musikalisches Zeitung with the famous quote about Chopin's genius talent.

> Eusebius recently came softly into the room. You know the ironic smile on that pate face; it is meant to awaken your curiosity. I was sitting at the piano with Florestan. Florestan, as you know, is one of those rare musical natures who seem to anticipate all that is imminent, new, or out of the ordinary. Yet today there was a surprise in store for him. With the words, "Hats off, gentlemen, a genius!" Eusebius produces a piece of music. He would not let us see the title. I turned the pages idly; this veiled enjoyment of soundless music has something magical about it. Besides, it seems to me that each composer has his individual note-patterns,

> recognizable to the eye: Beethoven looks different than Mozart, on paper. But now it seemed to me as if strange eyes, flower eyes, basilisk eyes, peacock eyes, maiden eyes were peeping up at me most wondrously; some parts seemed clearer—I thought I could detect Mozart's "Là ci darem la mano" entwined through a hundred chords. (1831)

Although pressed by Elsner and others to write a national opera, Chopin responded to his teacher that he preferred the career of a pianist. Opera was popular with aristocratic Polish audiences, and through allegory and folk influences could more effectively express patriotic feelings. The reception of a national sentiment is subjective and dependent on the background of the listener. At the same time, the composer's intention may not coincide completely with audience reaction. The view of the 19th-century music scholar Fredrick Niecks on national characteristics in Chopin's music underscored the need to assess nationalism in Chopin's music from varying perspectives.

> There are people who imagine that the difficulties of Chopin's music arise from its Polish national characteristics, and that to the Poles themselves it is as easy as their mother tongue; this, however, is a mistake. In fact, other countries had to teach Poland what is due to Chopin. That the aristocracy of Paris, Polish and native, did not comprehend the whole Chopin, although it may have appreciated and admired his sweetness, elegance, and exquisiteness, has been remarked by Liszt, an eye and ear-witness and an excellent judge. (Frederik Niecks, *Chopin, as a Man and Musician*, 3rd ed. 1902, p. 159)

In 1832, Chopin continued to make his way as a pianist. Arranging concerts in Paris took as long as two months. Two concerts were canceled, but introduced to aristocratic circles by émigré Polish nobility, Chopin attracted private music students; aside from Delfina Potocka, he also taught Lady Pauline Plater, as well as

Natalia and Ludmiła Komar. His first Paris concert held on February 26, where he presented the *Concerto in E minor* and *Variations Op. 2*, was a financial failure due to his limited exposure among Parisian audiences. A performance of Beethoven's *Ninth Symphony* in April made a profound artistic impression on Chopin. At a benefit concert for the poor on May 20 at the Conservatoire, he played the first movement of the *E Minor Concerto*. He began socializing with Polish émigré artists and literary figures as well as Parisian musicians, and by the end of 1832, publishing opportunities had increased, leading to greater exposure. His activities continued, with performances at musical events with local musicians and presentations of his own works for small salon gatherings.

Benefitting from the intellectual life of Paris, Chopin became well known among the aristocracy for his piano virtuosity, and was distinguished socially for his manners, bearing, and refinement. After 1833, he composed and published steadily. His music was more or less simultaneously published in France, Germany, and England. According to Jeffrey Kallberg, Chopin published internationally to increase his income and avoid the distribution of pirated versions of his music. His principal publishers were Maurice Schlesinger in France, Breitkopf und Härtel in Germany, and Christian Rudolph Wessel in England. Chopin transmitted his compositions to the publishers through manuscripts in his or a copyist's hand, proof sheets or plates from the French edition. The sources for his various publications, autograph manuscripts, fair copies, and printer's copies can be researched on the website of the Frédéric Chopin Society in Warsaw, www.chopin.nifc.pl/chopin.

Engaging in Parisian concert life was an equal priority. The piano compositions flowed from his pen. Although the *Allgemeine Musikalische Zeitung*, for example, printed helpful notices of his music, not all reviews were positive. Ludwig Rellstab, the editor of the music journal *Iris*, became a constant critic of Chopin's musical works, claiming that they were too original and too difficult for the hands.

> In search of ear-rendering dissonances, torturous transitions, sharp modulations, repugnant contortions of melody and rhythm, Chopin is altogether indefatigable. All that one can chance upon, is here brought forward to produce the effect of bizarre originality, especially the strangest tonalities, the most unnatural chord positions, the most preposterous combinations in regard to fingering. But it is not really worth the trouble to hold such long philippics for the same of the perverse Mazurkas of Herr Chopin. Had he submitted this music to a teacher, the latter, it is to be hoped, would have torn it up and thrown it at his feet–and this is what we symbolically wish to do. (*Iris*, Berlin, July 5,1833)

Along with the musical and social engagements came changes in his residence, first to 4 rue Cité Bergère in the summer of 1832, and then to 5, Chausée d'Anton the following June. In the summer of 1833, he vacationed at Franchômme's home in Le Côteau. Among the works he composed in 1833 were the *Mazurkas*, Op. 17 and *Nocturnes*, Op. 27. The nocturnes are mood pieces with lyric melodic lines. Irregular rhythmic patterns cause some ambiguity in the melodic structure. The Op. 27 *Nocturnes* are among Chopin's best works.

The *Mazurkas*, Op. 17 present accent patterns that reinforce the characteristic mazurka rhythm of a dotted note on the first beat, placing the stress on the second of three beats per measure. Several in the collection exhibit a drone effect consistent with the instrumental support of Polish folk music, and the foot stomp of the dance can be found represented by rhythmic accent and melodic leap. Along with increased harmonic ambiguity, the collection reveals Chopin's advancing concept of these Polish folk-influenced pieces. With the repeat of the balanced phrases, the melodies are varied with pianistic filigree. From a formal perspective, the ABA repetition pattern of earlier works is maintained.

In January 1834, Chopin met the Italian composer Vincenzo Bellini

(1801-1835) in the salon of the singer Lina Freppa. A line has been drawn between Chopin's melodies and the vocal style of Bellini. Chopin's closest friends at the time included Hector Berlioz, Franz Liszt, and Ferdinand Hiller. Given Chopin's association with other musicians, the exchange of stylistic trends is not surprising.

In the spring, Jan Matuszyński (1808-1842), a childhood friend who was a frequent correspondent, came to Paris and lived with Chopin at Rue Chausée d'Antin No. 5. Matuszyński worked in Paris as a physician, having received his medical training in Tubingen. As close friends who had been separated for five years, they attended theater and other events together. In December, Berlioz enlisted Chopin to play the slow movement of the *Concerto in E minor* at a benefit concert for Harriet Smithson (1800-1854), a Shakespearean actress and Berlioz's wife. On Christmas Day, Chopin performed in another benefit concert in the Salle Pleyel, playing several works with Liszt. With such a concentration of works for the piano, Chopin's father urged him to compose another concerto, but the petitions were futile, and we are left with only the two early works in this genre.

During the summer of 1835, Chopin vacationed in Enghien near Paris. He also visited the estate in Saint-Gratien belonging to Marquis Astolphe de Custine (1790-1857), a music lover and friend. A French aristocrat, the Marquis is known for his travel writing relating his impressions of a trip to Russia in the insightful book, *La Russie en 1839*. Later that summer, Chopin met with his parents in Karlsbad, also traveling to Dresden and Leipzig. Although working with a variety of publishers, he approached Breitkopf und Härtel to publish *the Polonaise in E flat Major*, Op. 22, *Études*, Op. 25, two *Polonaises*, Op. 26, and *Nocturnes*, Op. 27.

Chopin's family, separated from him by political geography, had remained foremost on his mind. He suffered from homesickness during the Christmas holidays each year. Reflecting this, the *Scherzo in B minor*, Op. 20 incorporates the Polish Christmas carol "Lulajże, Jezuniu." The death of his sister Emilia at age 14 in 1827 had a deep impact on him, and he always remembered the anniversary of her passing. His many letters to family attest to his devotion to their wellbeing. On November 22, 1832, his sister Ludwika had married József Kalasanty Jędrzejewicz. With regard to the engagement, Chopin wrote to his new brother-in-law:

> You tell me the news I longed for! I have always been fond of you, have always felt as a friend to you, and be assured that you will now find in me the person you ought to find. I would give half my life to be able to embrace you both on your wedding day and see you at the altar; but that cannot be; I can only send you, as you ask, a polonaise and a mazur, so that you can hop about and be really gay and that your souls may rejoice. (September 10, 1832)

On November 8, 1834, there was another family celebration in Poland when his sister Izabella married Antoni Barciński.

When he met with his parents in the summer of 1835, he notated the refrain from the future (and current) Polish national anthem, "Jeszcze Polska nie zginęła" ("Poland hasn't perished yet") in the album of Konstanty Młokosiewicz, a Lieutenant in the Hussars. With his parents, he visited the Duczyn estate of Count Thum-Hohenstein, parents of his Parisian students. On September 19, 1835, while in Dresden, he became acquainted with Maria Wodzińska through her family, since he was friends with her brothers and had visited them in Służewo. This led to a romantic relationship with Maria, the second of three over the course of Chopin's life. During the following months, he often met in Paris with Antoni Wodziński, Maria's brother. Chopin's return to Paris in the fall of 1835 was interrupted by his illness with coughing fits; the coughing up of blood that started as early as 1831 continued. Incapacitated on his return trip, he stayed for a time in Heidelberg with his student Adolphe Gutmann (1819-1882) but was able to return to Paris on October 20. Gutmann, who came to Paris to study with Chopin and another émigré composer, Julian Fontana, served as a copyist of a number of Chopin's works. He also delivered letters to Chopin's family.

As a guest at many musical soirées in Paris, Chopin expressed his Polish identity by improvising at the piano to poems of Polish literary figures such as Wincenty Pol (1807-1872) and Adam Mickiewicz (1798-1855), Poland's greatest Romantic poet, as well as creating impromptu variations on Polish melodies. Focused on composing and publishing his music, he again was recognized by Robert Schumann in the *Neue Zeitschrift für Musik* on April 22, 1836, with an enthusiastic review of the two piano concertos. In August 1836, his meeting with the parents of Maria Wodzińska during his month's stay in Marienbad led to an engagement in September, but the marriage was conditional on the improvement of Chopin's health, so the arrangement was kept private. In the next year, Chopin continued corresponding with Maria's mother, but letters from Maria became increasingly superficial and impersonal. The engagement lasted only a year. But despite this personal setback, Chopin remained active, as indicated by his comments on his daily schedule:

> Why must it be twelve already? At twelve I have to give a lesson and to keep on till six; then dinner, and after that to an evening in society, till 11. (November 1, 1836)

Moving on to Leipzig in September 1836, he met with Robert and Clara Schumann, along with their musical circle. The following summer his health worsened.

Meeting George Sand

It was at the end of October 1836 at the salon of Countess Marie d'Agoult that Chopin met Aurore Dudevant, widely known as George Sand. Countess d'Agoult, also known as the literary figure Daniel Stern, was Liszt's lover at the time. According to Liszt (1811-1836), the pianist and composer who wrote an early biography of Chopin, Sand wanted to meet the Polish composer. Initial impressions were not favorable, and in a letter to Ferdinand Hiller Chopin wrote: "What an unpleasant woman!" Yet, that winter he socialized with Sand, Liszt, and Countess d'Agoult, and met with other Polish émigrés. Sand was an independent woman, clearly a slave to her passions. Indicative of her posture of role reversal, she dressed like a "literary school boy."

At that time, he also developed a business relationship with the Parisian piano manufacturer Pleyel, and in 1837 Chopin traveled with Camille Pleyel (1788-1855) to London, where he worked on his music publishing relations. Chopin even sent a Pleyel piano to the Wodzińskis before the breaking of the engagement. Later in 1837, he declined invitations from George Sand to literary events and to vacation at her summer estate in Nohant.

Works composed during this period included the *Impromptu* Op. 29, which stands out from other impromptus for variety and expansion of the three-part form. The Opus 30 *Mazurkas* continue the pattern of pieces in ternary form with regular, repeated phrases in simple texture. Some incorporations of modal elements highlight the reflection of Polish folk music. The mazurka rhythm persists with the initial beats of the measure bouncing off the final 16th note. In the Op. 33 collection, the tempos vary, phrases transition to different key levels, melodic shifts between registers create a call and response, and Lydian inflections add to the folk dance effect. The *Mazurkas*, Op. 41, are more experimental with disruptions of the triple meter and drifting of the melody to inner voices of the texture. The sets of *Mazurkas* Opp. 30, 33, and 41 continue the infusion of folk elements such as bourdon pedals, drone effects, rhythmic accents related to the dance, and Lydian modality in the melodic lines. The four *Mazurkas*, Op. 68, continue the incorporation of Polish folk elements, especially the drone effect adopted from Polish folk instruments, such as the duda or bagpipe. The *Mazurka*, Op. 68, no. 2 is a familiar piece with alternating major and minor phrases. The concluding pieces of the collection display the drone effect and chordal harmony as contrast.

As Chopin continued to compose and perform, press reviews became more divided. Nevertheless, his reputation as a pianist grew through his composed works and improvisations. Additionally, he wrote songs and improvised to the poetry of his Polish compatriots. As Sand continued to pursue Chopin, a romance developed between them, which reached a climax in the fall of 1838 with their stay in Mallorca. The artist Eugene Delacroix (1798-1863) sketched a joint portrait that summer. Chopin and Sand gathered artists and musicians at her home and shared with a slate of friends. These interactions with the Polish émigrés resulted in stories in the French press about conditions in Poland. He continued to stay in Mallorca throughout the winter of 1838-39. The trip was kept secret from all but a few friends. Sand wanted to take her son Maurice to this Spanish island for its more favorable climate, but for Chopin, funding such an excursion was an issue. Yet, as he expressed in his letter to Julian Fontana on November 19, 1838, Mallorca promised to improve his spirits, with its sun-drenched sea and mountains, as well as rich greenery. Intended to improve his health, in reality, the trip exacerbated Chopin's illness.

In all, the trip to Mallorca was not an enjoyable experience. Writing about the stay in her book *Un Hiver à Majorque*, Sand discussed the land and the local culture, history, and economy. The travelers did not find the island's residents to be hospitable, probably because they believed Chopin to be contagious with pulmonary consumption. By December 18, the Parisian visitors were able to move to a monastery at Valldemossa, where Chopin had use of the Pleyel piano shipped to him and received after extended negotiations were completed with the customs officials. Due to the hardships of living in damp conditions, Chopin's health declined over the winter. In her book, Sand referred to him as "the invalid."

Remarkably, given his declining health, Chopin managed to compose some of his most innovative compositions during that trip. Writing to Julian Fontana from Palma on December 14, 1838, he described his devotion to his creative efforts while enduring rustic accommodations.

> Tomorrow I go to that wonderful monastery of Valdemosa, to write in the cell of some old monk, who perhaps had more

> fire in his soul than I, and stifled it, stifled and extinguished it, because he had it in vain. (14 December 1838)

In many respects, the winter in Mallorca was not the idyllic experience he or Sand envisioned. They did not feel welcome on the island and struggled to understand the local culture. Together with Chopin's ill health, this placed a strain on a relationship that might not have endured were it not for their artistic connection.

4. Chopin and Sand 1839-1847

Chopin's relationship with George Sand and her family was as complex as any in modern times. Although Chopin and Sand had an artistic connection, they were opposites in their personalities, but their differences complemented each other.

In February 1839, Chopin became seriously ill in Mallorca and relocated to Barcelona. By May, he again was traveling and crossed the Mediterranean to visit Genoa, Italy, later returning west for a stay in the French city of Marseilles. On May 22, he departed from Marseilles to spend the summer months at Sand's summer home in Nohant, where she had planned to teach her children. Arriving on June 3, he slowly recovered from his illness and devoted his time to composing piano music in an assortment of genres—nocturnes, mazurkas, the *Ballade in F Major*, Op. 38, and *Sonata in B-flat minor*, Op. 35.

Although Chopin flirted with sonata form in various guises throughout his career, there are only a few works with that title. Distinctive about the *Piano Sonata*, Op. 35 in the broad view is that the scherzo is placed as the second movement, rather than the third, which is more typical of a sonata-based cycle. It might be noted that Dobrzyński, another student of Elsner, resorted to the same format. The third movement of the Op. 35 *Sonata* is the well-known "Funeral March." Beethoven's *Piano Sonata*, Op. 26, a work that Chopin knew well, presents a scherzo as the second movement and a funeral march as the third. Otherwise, Chopin's *Second Sonata* reflects the approach he took to sonata form in other works. The first movement follows a traditional sonata form outline, although with the second theme contrasting greatly with the agitated beginning. The return of the second theme in the tonic at the conclusion of the movement resolves the tension created by changes in key throughout the piece. The somber "Funeral March" was actually composed first, and other movements added in relation to it.

The larger-scale works of the period are some of the most performed and highly appreciated of Chopin's oeuvre. The *Scherzo*, Op. 39 explores the range of the piano with scale passages in octaves. The four ballades provide an interesting view of Chopin's creative thought, and their intriguing design has had a varied analytical history. Earlier theorists struggled to fit the contrasting sections of the ballades into a traditional sonata form mold. An alternative view places consideration on the narrative nature of the compositions. In the context of the 19th-century Polish culture concentrated in a sizable émigré community situated in Paris, connections have been suggested between Chopin's musical ballades and the literary ballades of Adam Mickiewicz. Penned by the most celebrated Polish literary figure of that time, Mickiewicz's messianic posture on the Polish nation had broad influence in the period after the 1830 November Insurrection. His Romantic vision was set earlier in *Konrad Wallenrod* (1826) and *Dziady* (1832), and Chopin's introspective compositions expressed a similar spirit. The Mickiewicz ballades seem a natural model for the Chopin pieces, even with the difficulty in relating literary expression to a non-textural musical work. One approach to understanding Chopin's ballads suggests that the contrasting musical themes are programmatic and tell an unstated story that guides the work. More recent musical analysis has considered the contrasting themes and key relations as a more complex adaptation of sonata form based on large-scale structural tension and release.

The second Ballade best lends itself to a narrative interpretation by dramatic insertion of popular musical styles. Musicologist Jonathan Bellman has analyzed the work as a narrative of Polish national martyrdom. This ballade suggests sonata form's thematic and tonal contrast, although the reprise of the themes is in reverse order. Interestingly, the work begins in F major but closes in A minor. The Op. 47 *Third Ballade* presents more complex musical thought, especially in its opening statements, and a greater departure from sonata form. With this ballade, there is a rapid acceleration toward the end when two initially separate ideas are fused together. This is typical of Chopin's mature works, which build excitement toward an ending with a prominent coda. In Op. 52, we see the two principal themes incorporate the rhythmic influence of the waltz and the use of more counterpoint. This late-style work treats the thematic material in variation as the piece progresses. The waltzes of Op. 64 were also composed during this period. Chopin's waltzes became popular because they were Central European in nature.

Defying explanation, the three innovative genres in Chopin's oeuvre each have four works. Composed along with the Ballades, the Scherzos of Chopin were conceived as extended works. Originally, scherzos appeared as more spirited movements in multi-movement compositions, replacing the minuet third movement. Chopin's scherzos are independent piano works structured in an underlying sonata form structure. The *Impromptu* Op. 36 departs from the three-part schemes of the other three Impromptus.

Derived from Chopin's early compositions based on an improvisatory approach to the presentation and development of thematic material, the *Fantasy*, Op. 49 and *Polonaise Fantasy*, Op. 61 also show a loose relation to sonata form. Yet, the contrasting sections follow a free sequence of musical ideas. The improvisatory elements alternate with theme and accompaniment, supporting a call and response pattern over the entire keyboard. The Op. 61 is a fully mature work, which underwent extensive revision before completion. The sketches reveal that parts were conceived in other keys. At this point in his creative life, Chopin searched for new methods of continuity. The dual-reference title reflects his changing view of musical genres. The work begins like improvisational passagework at the piano, but then settles into the polonaise rhythm. According to Kallberg, "Chopin redefined his principles of musical form in the *Polonaise-Fantasy*. In doing so, he established the basic mission for what was to be his new- and last-style."

In response to the important place the Polish homeland had in Chopin's life, the polonaises continued to capture the spirit of the nation under partition, both for those remaining in Polish territories and the émigré community abroad. The change to more strongly affirm a Polish national identity can be perceived with the two Polonaises of Op. 26, composed between 1831 and 1836. The later *Polonaise*, Op. 40, No. 1 "The Military," exudes a heroic sound that ensured its popularity and reference in Jerzy Andrzejewski's 1948 novel *Ashes and Diamonds*. The Op. 44 *Polonaise*, also popular, is developmental in melodic approach, while maintaining the polonaise rhythm in the left hand. The middle section moves to a "Tempo di Mazurka." Simple in form, it follows the traditional three-part sectional layout. The *Polonaise* Op. 53, based on a similar dance rhythm, has a comparable structure with a basso ostinato. Beginning with a bravura introduction, the principal theme is repeated at the octave with the polonaise rhythm in the left hand. This A-flat polonaise was a symbol of liberty to those with Polish sentiments. The Opp. 40 and 53 works were often performed in 19th-century Poland and admired by critics.

In August 1839, Chopin studied the preludes and fugues of Johann Sebastian Bach's *Well-Tempered Clavier*, the work of a composer he regarded highly, and published the *Preludes*, Op. 28. Although completed in Mallorca, the set of 24 *Preludes*, one of Chopin's most important collections, engaged the composer's creativity beginning in 1836. This collection of piano miniatures reflects Bach's influence in its organizational concept of presenting a piece in each major and minor key. However, the intention of the title "prelude" remains speculative because the pieces are not specifically related to other compositions for which they would serve as introductory statements. Nonetheless, their melodic and harmonic structure have intrigued generations of analysts. From the piano figuration, often suggesting improvisation, linear melodies emerge to focus the texture. The tonal ambiguity in many of the miniatures has led to a variety of interpretations. In the words of author Jim Samson, "By far the most compelling and certainly the most influential body of analytical studies of Chopin is to be found in the writings of Heinrich Schenker." Schenkerian analysis works well for Chopin because, as Jim Samson has stated, harmony is "one of the principal shaping elements in much of his music, but a distinction between structural and 'contrapuntal' harmonies is central to his musical thought." Schenkerian analysis, as applied with good results to a number of the preludes, has heightened our understanding of Chopin's approach to musical form.

By the end of October, Chopin had returned to a new apartment in Paris, at 5, rue Tronchet, with Sand moving nearby, to 16, rue Pigalle. During the following year, he lived with Sand in Paris, continuing to teach private students and compose. During this period, he expanded his group of friends and began his acquaintance with Ignaz Moscheles (1794-1870), another touring pianist. He first met the mezzo-soprano Pauline Viardot-Garcia (1821-1910) at the end of August 1840, and the two became close friends. When attending musical events during this period, he was often accompanied by Sand. In December, they attended rehearsals for Mozart's *Requiem* and lectures by Adam Mickiewicz at the College de France.

Chopin continued composing while living with Sand. In his typical working process, he created his compositions at the keyboard and then notated sketches hurriedly on paper. His interactions with poets and literary figures from Poland is reflected in his music through dedications and song texts. Reluctant to perform in large gatherings, he appeared as a pianist at limited private events. At the end of June 1840, he performed a private recital at St. Gratien, the estate of Marquis de Custine.

In July 1840, Chopin corresponded with his Warsaw mentor, Józef Elsner, about the complications in seeking a publisher for Elsner's *Oratorio*. Chopin related that extended works had a high cost for publication and did not sell because they were only performed at the Conservatoire. Additionally, the music performed at the Conservatoire did not often include new works. "The Conservatoire sets the tone for greater music; therefore, a publisher can count only on what the Conservatoire will bring in." (July 24, 1840)

Love and music

At the beginning of 1841, Sand began publishing in serial format the account of their winter in Mallorca, Un hiver a Majorique, in the Revue des deux mondes. The music Chopin composed on the Spanish island–études, preludes, nocturnes, mazurkas, and ballades–was presented in a recital for selected concertgoers at the Salle Pleyel on April 26. Parisian society filled the audience, along with Polish compatriots, poets Mickiewicz and Stefan Witwicki.

That summer, from June 18 to November 4, he vacationed with Sand, her family, and friends at Nohant. Pauline Viardot spent two weeks there singing bel canto arias and Spanish folk songs. Chopin's long interest in folk music continued, and he spent time that summer transcribing folk dances, bourees (French dances and music), and bagpipe tunes at village events. Chopin spent three to four months at Nohant each summer from 1838 to 1846, except in1840. It was through Sand that Chopin knew Eugene Delacroix, the artist responsible for one of the well-known portraits of the composer. Sand kept an open house for friends, which accumulated considerable expense. At the end of the summer period, the Parisian papers would announce Chopin's return to the city.

He was prolific, completing several compositions, including the Allegro de Concert. This piece had been sketched years earlier as the beginning of a third concerto. Chopin resisted applying programmatic titles to his piano compositions, although requested to do so by his publishers. In October and November of 1841, after returning to Paris, he published all the pieces he wrote at Nohant, Opp. 43-49. In Paris again, he lived at 16, rue Pigalle in a separate apartment, but near Sand. On December 2 of that year, he performed at a white-tie concert at the royal court in the Tuileries. He sent a gift of an elegant dinner service to his family in Poland.

After seven summers spent at Nohant, Chopin was an intimate member of Sand's family and inner circle. The letters show his relationship with Sand's children—Solange and Maurice. As a writer, Sand adopted Chopin, and their relationship became a subject for her writing.

On February 21, 1842, Chopin gave his annual concert at the Salle Pleyel with Pauline Viardot and August Franchômme, close friends and accomplished musicians. The program included an assortment of genres—nocturnes, preludes, mazurkas, and impromptus. It was said that Chopin's performance did not bring out the sound sufficiently for large-scale concerts. Although he had limited income from musical activities, he spent on indulgences and non-essentials, as well as on contributions to support to poor Poles. April 20 marked the death from tuberculosis of his close friend and frequent correspondent Jan Matuszyński. Paris was where he spent his time teaching and socializing; Nohant was where he devoted himself to composition.

Although his creative production diminished between 1842 and 1847, this period marked the advancement and cohesion of Chopin's musical style in a number of genres. The *Nocturne*, Op. 48, No. 1 presents a musical parallelism in its formal structure, and a section of complex chordal writing. It also exhibits the funeral march mood that is better expressed in the *B-minor Sonata*. The mazurkas of this period became more expressive and introspective. Examples of folk elements, such as bourdon pedals creating a drone effect, and use of the Phrygian mode abound in Op. 41. In the Opp. 50 and 56, we find less emphasis on Polish elements and movement toward a more expressive range. The three mazurkas of Opus 50 feature sections of contrasting texture, melody in the lower sounding left-hand part, or thick chordal sections, as well as simple melody and accompaniment. The *Mazurkas*, Op. 59 have a simpler texture, with differentiated melody and accompaniment.

Returning to Paris on October 10, Chopin moved to 9, Square

d'Orléans, while Sand resided at no. 5. From here, Chopin continued to attract piano students; teaching piano was his primary means of support. The musical evenings, hosted by Sand, continued through the fall with a variety of artistic guests in attendance, including Honoré de Balzac (1799-1850), Adam Mickiewicz (1798-1855), Stefan Witwicki (1801-1847), Wojciech Grzymała (1793-1871), Pierre Leroux (1797-1871), Emmanuel Arago (1812-1896), Louis Blanc (1811-1882), Hector Berlioz (1803-1869), Franz Liszt (1811-1886), Giacomo Meyerbeer (1791-1864), Auguste Franchômme (1808-1884), Adolf Gutmann (1819-1882), Pauline Viardot (1821-1910), Marie d'Agoult (1805-1876), Eugene Delacroix (1788-1863), and others.

At this point in his teaching career, Chopin was able to witness the public performance of his students. Twelve-year-old prodigy, Carl Filtsch, performed the *Concerto in E minor* on November 28, 1842, and the next January he played at Baron James de Rothschild's (1792-1868) home with Chopin at the second piano. As his composition and publications activities continued, Chopin benefited from a fourth summer at Nohant, and returned to Paris on October 29 with Maurice Sand. Although sick and under a doctor's care, he took on new students and performed at the Rothschild's salon on November 15. Chopin's correspondence includes many reports of what he heard at the opera and in concert, as well as social activities with his artistic acquaintances. He was closest to his Polish friends and cellist Auguste Franchômme.

Chopin was actively engaged in the publication of his compositions. On December 15, 1842, he wrote to his publishers, Breitkopf und Härtel:

> Gentlemen,
> I have to offer you a Scherzo (for 600 fr.), a Ballade (for 600 fr.), a Polonaise (500 fr.).
> Besides these I have written an Impromptu, of several pages, which I do not even offer to you, as I wish to oblige one of my old acquaintances, who for the last two years has been constantly asking me for something for Herr

Hofmeister. I mention it in order to explain to you my motive in this matter.

Imagine his disappointment when this *Impromptu* was released publically in print. From Nohant in July of 1843, he wrote to music editor Maurice Schlesinger:

> Dear Friend!
>
> In the *Impromptu* which you have issued in the Gazette of June 9th the pages are wrongly numbered, which renders my composition incomprehensible. Though I am far from the meticulousness which our friend Moscheles shows with regard to his works, I still feel it my duty to your subscribers to ask you to insert in the next number the following *erratum*:
>
> Page 3: read p. 5
>
> Page 5: read p. 3 (July, 22, 1843)

In December, he executed a global contract (except for France and Great Britain) with Breitkopf und Härtel for an entire group of pieces.

> I, the undersigned, domiciled in Paris at rue St. Lazare No. 34, acknowledge that I have sold to Messrs. Breitkopf and Haertel in [Leipzig] the rights of the following works composed by me; namely
>
> [List of works, included]
>
> I declare that I have ceded this property to the said firm, with reserve or time limit and for all countries except France and England, and I acknowledge that I have received the price agreed upon, for which a separate receipt has been given.
>
> F. Chopin
>
> Paris, 10 December 1843

By this point, he had also published with other music producers, including Friedrich Kistner, C.F. Peters, Friedrich Hofmeister,

Maurice Schlesinger, Julius Schuberth, and Pietro Mechetti. Still cherishing his connection to Polish culture, he and Sand attended the Polish bazaar organized by Princess Anne Czartoryska after Christmas. The Czartoryskis were an old Polish noble family who were Chopin's patrons. The center of their activities in Paris was the Hôtel Lambert. Marcelina Czartoryska was Chopin's student.

Despite off-and-on health problems, Chopin continued to perform short concerts and support his students. As had been the pattern, he spent the summer of 1844 with Sand at Nohant, where he could devote himself to composing. In August, he was visited there by his older sister Ludwika and her husband. With business in Paris, Chopin returned to the city to once again bid farewell to his sister before the couple's return to Poland.

There is some question on how well known Chopin's music was in his native country during his lifetime. Commenting on his publishing, Chopin intimated on the availability of his compositions in Poland:

> My new mazurkas have come out in Berlin at Stern's, so I don't know whether they will reach you; you, who in Warsaw generally get your music from [Leipzig]. Letter to his family, December 12, 1845.

References in Polish publications of the period reveal some attention to Chopin's residence in Paris at the time, but with distant communication during tenuous times in Europe, Warsaw remained somewhat isolated. Concomitantly, the interests of other Polish intellectuals of the period seemed to be drifting in these years. In a letter to Stefan Witwicki at Easter in 1845, Chopin related:

> What shall I tell you: that tomorrow, Monday, is the Easter festival at Prince Czartoryski's; that Mickiewicz is not lecturing this year; that many of his followers are abandoning him; that it is said they have written apologies to His Majesty. But what is grievous is that 2 (it is said that Pilichowski is one of them) signed documents before

a notary, giving themselves into subjection, like property, like slaves, to Towianski. [a Messianist religious leader]... In a word: disputes; so no doubt it will come to a melancholy end.

When illness did not inhibit his activities, Chopin attended major performances with Sand and others in their circle. Most of his own concerts were held at private soirees, often with a Polish connection in the relationships. During the summer of 1845 at Nohant, Chopin began teaching Sand's daughter, Solange, to play the piano, but serious disagreements emerged among Chopin, Sand, and her son, Maurice. As mentioned in his letters, his longing for family in Poland intensified. He returned to Paris at the end of November, and his memories of home stimulated the desire to experience traditional Polish Christmas celebrations. The news that he exchanged with his family in Poland reveals Chopin's widespread intellectual interests. Writing from Nohant on October 11, 1846, he shared:

> Among other news, you have probably already heard of M. Leverrier's new planet. Leverrier, of the Paris observatory, noticing certain irregularities in the planet Uranus, ascribed them to some other planet, still unknown, and described its distance, direction, size: in a word, everything, just as Galle in Berlin and–[Adam] in London have now observed it. What a triumph for science, to be able to arrive at such a discovery by means of calculation.

Continuing his social life after a bout of illness, Chopin once again spent the summer of 1846–his last–at Nohant. Typical of the summer schedule, there was a succession of guests. Sand's caricature of Chopin in her 1846 novel *Lucretia Floriani* caused mutual disillusionment about their relationship. The resemblance of the character Prince Karol to Chopin seemed obvious to many, but perhaps not to Chopin himself. At the opening of the novel, Prince Karol de Roswald is described by Sand as having been "weak and ailing" as a child, and continuing to have "delicate health."

On the one hand he saw innate aristocracy, distinction of intelligence, purity of morals and nobility of instincts, and he said to himself "Let me be with them." On the other hand he saw degradation, baseness, mental instability, but he did not say "Let me join them, to redeem them, if possible." No, he had been taught to say "They are doomed. Let us give them food and clothes, but let us not compromise ourselves by contact with them. They are hardened and sullied; let us abandon their souls to the mercy of God."

Returning to Paris alone, Chopin continued his teaching, composing and publishing. It was around that time that Louis-August Bisson (1814-1876) made his well-known portrait of the composer using an early photographic method known as daguerreotype—a process combining an iodine-sensitized silvered plate and mercury vapor.

Throughout this period of his life, Chopin remained interested in Polish musical life and musician friends from his formative period. Chopin wrote to Józef Nowakowski, who apparently was in Paris in 1847:

> You know that it is difficult for me to leave the house, and if you have not much pleasure in seeing me, I have much in seeing you, and that for no other reason than just because you are the same person as in the old days at home, and such an original as no other under the sun. When once you leave here, even if you were to pay for it we shan't see each other any more. Afterwards you'll be sorry that you didn't give me a sight of your whiskers again.

The social and musical calendar continued in the winter of 1847. Returning to writing for the violoncello, Chopin completed the *Cello Sonata* and presented the first performance with Franchômme. The work was performed in March of that year for the Czartoryskis. Chopin remained connected to Polish music by receiving recent musical publications from his family. With regard to his Parisian family life, Chopin had misgivings about the acceptance of the sculptor and painter Auguste Clésinger (1814-1883) as Solange's future husband, and this was the source of much of the disagreement with Sand. In May of that year, Solange's wedding proceeded during a period of illness for Chopin. The conflict about Solange caused the final separation from Sand, codified in a letter to Chopin dated July 28. By Christmas, Chopin commented: "[Solange] was in Nohant with the Duvernets; but her Mother received her coldly, and told her that if she will leave her husband she can come back to Nohant."

Chopin continued to compose and attend Parisian soirées. He later housed Solange and Clésinger when Sand sent them out. She gave up her Paris apartments in 1847 and spent the winter of 1847-48 at Nohant.

Chopin's last Paris concert in the Salle Pleyel was held on February 16, 1848, for an exclusive audience of 300 aristocrats and artistic elites. Along with Chopin, other performers participated in the event, as noted in an enthusiastic review. Chopin contributed by performing in a Mozart trio and presenting an array of his own compositions: nocturne, étude, berceuse, sonata movement, preludes, mazurkas, and waltz.

5. Illness and Final Years 1848

The year 1848 brought political upheaval to Europe and with it a diminishing of Chopin's income from piano lessons. In France, revolutionary activity ended the constitutional monarchy of Louis-Philippe, resulting in a government headed by Louis-Napoleon.

Chopin's letter to Julian Fontana (April 4, 1848) expressed his concern about the situation in partitioned Poland.

> What the papers all write here is all lies. There is no republic in Cracow, nor has the Austrian emperor called himself king of Poland, and in the Lwów papers, in the address to the Stadion, no one asks him to do so, as quoted here. The King of Prussia also has no particular thought of getting rid of Poznań. He made himself a laughingstock at home; but in spite of that, the Poznań Germans write him addresses, saying that: "as this land was won by the blood of their fathers, and as they do not even know Polish, they declare that they do not wish to be under any other government than the Prussian." All this, you see, smells of war, and where it will start, no one can tell.

As a response to the unrest in France, Chopin went to England and stayed there from April 20 to November 23, teaching and giving concerts, both for aristocrats in private salons and in public. After arriving in England, he played for Lady Gainsborough and Marquis Douglas. In May 1848, he became acquainted with the well-known vocalist Jenny Lind. In the same month, he performed for Count Sutherland, and on June 23, for Lady Sartoris. On July 7, 1848, he gave a concert for Lord Falmouth with Pauline Viardot-Garcia. On this English tour, Chopin seemed more comfortable than in Paris performing for large audiences.

In August, Chopin left London for a couple of weeks to stay in Scotland with the family of Jane Stirling (1804-1859), one of his piano students. Through the remainder of this tour, he appeared in concerts in Manchester, Glasgow, and Edinburgh, and on November 16, he gave a public performance for veterans of the November Insurrection. He returned to Paris on November 24.

The busyness of the London trip was overwhelming. As he wrote to his student Adolf Gutmann on May 5, 1848,

> Erard was very courteous, and placed a piano at my disposal. I have one instrument of Broadwood and one of Pleyel: three in all; but what is the use, when I have not the time to play on them. I have innumerable visits to pay, and my days flash past like lightning. Today I have not had one free moment of time to write to Pleyel.

The trip to London underscored to Chopin the differences in England's artistic culture as compared to the artistic ethos on the continent.

> Art, here, means painting, sculpture and architecture. Music is not an art and is not called art; and if you say an artist, an Englishman understands that as meaning a painter, architect or sculptor. Music is a profession, not an art, and no one speaks or writes of any musician as an artist, for in their language and customs it is something else than art; it is a *profession*. (October 21, 1848)

In his final year, as his health continued to deteriorate, Chopin reduced the number of piano lessons he taught. In June, his sister Ludwika arrived with her husband once again in response to his worsening health. "If you can, do come. I am ill, and no doctor will help me as much as some of you." (June 22, 1849) In the midst of consultations about his illness, diagnosed as tuberculosis, Chopin moved from Square d'Orléans to 12, Place Vendôme. By September, he was bedridden, but received students and friends at his bedside. When he died on October 17, 1849, sculptor Auguste Clésinger made his death mask. On October 30, Mozart's *Requiem* was performed at his funeral in St. Madeleine Church in Paris. Appropriate as this musical selection was to the occasion, this choral masterwork was clearly a favorite of Chopin. Writing to Mlle de Rozières from Nohant on Pentecost in 1846, only two years before his death, Chopin urged:

> If you are ever sending anything here, would you please include my little score of the Mozart Requiem, which I left at No. 5 (or No. 9), and which is with the Stabat.

Through the course of his life, Chopin had lost his love relationship and companionship with George Sand, the freedom of his Polish home, and of course, his health. Burial ceremonies were held at Père-Lachaise Cemetery to the accompaniment of the "Funeral March" from the *Sonata in B-flat Minor*.

6. Chopin's Legacy

Chopin, like some other Polish Romantic artists—including Adam Mickiewicz and poet, dramatist, painter, and sculptor, Cyprian Norwid—left Poland as a young man, settling in Paris.

Norwid, who was Chopin's friend in exile, penned a lasting tribute to the composer, aptly named "Chopin's Piano:"

La musique est une chose étrange! – Byron [Music is a strange thing!]

L'art? ... c'est l'art – et puis, Voilà tout. – Béranger [Art?...It's art – and then, that's all]

1
Bound to your place those penultimate days
Whose plot was impenetrable –
– Myth-full,
Dawn-pallid ...
– Life's end a whisper summons its start:
"I will not render you – no! I will raise you! ..."

In Poland, Chopin has been considered a bard, a national symbol, a youth inspired by the nation's folklore, and a prophet of philosophical depth. Author Jim Samson discussed three Chopin myths: the salon composer, the Romantic composer, and the Slavonic composer. A number of scholarly articles have explored Chopin's relationship with prominent literary figures. His legacy, as intimated by Norwid, continues long after the composer's death. In the simplest of terms, Chopin's influence has been perpetuated in the genres of his life's work—mazurkas, polonaises, nocturnes, and, to a lesser degree, preludes, scherzos, waltzes—all taken up by composers who followed.

Chopin's legacy intensified in the 20th century. The importance of his keyboard style on composers of piano music such as Alexander Scriabin and Sergei Rachmaninoff cannot be underestimated. Numerous musical theorists and analysts have isolated passages in their music that reflect deep knowledge of Chopin's music. Chopin also had a profound impact on prominent Polish composers such as Karol Szymanowski (1882-1937) and Witold Lutoslawski (1913-1994).

Inspired by Polish folk music, Szymanowski revered Chopin's works. He wrote a number of essays on the impact and importance of Chopin's music, emphasizing the universal aspects of Chopin's art. According to Szymanowski, "Chopin infused a 'primitive, spontaneous 'Polishness' into art music." These comments accompanied a political climate of renewal in Polish nationalism in the aftermath of World War I, but also a period of conflicting views of Poland's political future. Szymanowski described Chopin's music as representing the ideal of the whole nation and having "that elevated position which is both Polish and universal, magically created in the noblest diamond of his music, shines with the clear, pure, unwavering light of truth, won by the unremitting effort of his own hands."

Although Chopin's music is judged for its universal appeal as Romantic art, and performed by pianists from all nations, scholarship on the composer and his creative work revolves around his native Poland. Indeed, other musicologists and theorists have published enlightening research on Chopin's music, but the scholarship emanating from Poland cannot be ignored. Nevertheless, when discussing why Chopin and his music were so infused in the national consciousness, there is value in varying perspectives. International congresses, typically scheduled around anniversary years, have provided a forum for sharing scholarly work with performance perspectives. In Poland's post-World War II socialist period, promotion of Chopin as a national icon supported ideological and political motives. The composer's reliance on folk sources for inspiration resonated with an ideological focus on the proletariat. Folk music and dance ensembles supported by the government were popular with citizens and foreigners alike.

In another realm, Chopin's music has accompanied dramatic sequences in numerous motion pictures, often where romantic introspection enhances the *mise en scène*. As a strange irony, the use of his works in TV and film might only be comparable to the popularity of the Mozart *Requiem*, especially the Lacrimosa, in the media. The Mozart *Requiem* and Chopin's "Funeral March" both have acquired dramatic associations beyond the intentions of their conception. And, of course, Chopin was long enamored of the Mozart work performed for his funeral.

The performance genealogy of prominent concert artists often can be traced back to Chopin and his teaching of piano techniques. Led by the Frederic Chopin Society's international piano competition held in Warsaw on a four-year cycle, piano competitions are held worldwide to identify and recognize outstanding performers of Chopin's music. The music lends itself to varying interpretations, making the display of insight and musicianship a key part of the judging.

And it is here that Chopin's legacy is most lasting; in performance by pianists of all skill levels, his music lives on!

Sources

Albán Juárez, Marita and Ewa Sławińska-Dahlig. *Chopin's Poland. A Guidebook to Places Associated with the Composer*. Trans. John Comber. Warsaw: NIFC, 2007.

Andrewjewski, Jerzy. *Ashes and Diamonds*. Writers from the Other Europe, ed. Philip Roth. New York: Penguin Books, 1980. Ashes and Diamonds, accessed August 5, 2017, https://www.youtube.com/watch?v=nIoFhwbhvrk.

Atwood, William G. *Fryderyk Chopin: Pianist from Warsaw*. New York: Columbia University Press, 1987.

Chopin.pl. Website of the Fryderyk Chopin Society/Towarszystwo im. Fryderyka Chopina in Warsaw, Poland. Accessed August 5, 2017 www.chopin,pl. 1997-.

Davies, Norman. *God's Playground: A History of Poland*. New York: Columbia University Press, 1982, 2 vols.

Eigeldinger, Jean-Jacques. *Chopin: Pianist and Teacher: As Seen by his Pupils*. Trans Naomi Shohet, with Krysia Osostowicz and Roy Howat. Cambridge and New York: Cambridge University Press, 1988.

Goldberg, Halina, ed. *The Age of Chopin: Interdisciplinary Inquiries*. Bloomington, IN: Indiana University Press, 2004.

Goldberg, Halina. "Chopin in Warsaw's Salons," *Polish Music Journal* 2, no. 1-2 (1999).

Goldberg, Halina. *Music in Chopin's Warsaw*. London and New York: Oxford University Press, 2008.

Kallberg, Jeffrey. *Chopin at the Boundaries: Sex, History, and Musical Genre*. Cambridge: Harvard University Press, 1996.

Kallberg, Jeffrey. "Chopin in the Marketplace: Aspects of the International Music Publishing Industry in the First Half of the Nineteenth Century." Notes 39, no. 3 (1983): 535-569; Notes 39, no. 4 (1983): 795-824.

Kieniewicz, Stefan. *Historia Polski 1795-1918*. Warsaw: Państwowe Wydawnictwo Naukowe, 1970.

Michałowski, Karol. *Karol Szymanowski*, vol. 1, Pisma muzyczne. Kraków: Polskie Wydawnictwo Muzyczne, 1984.

Narodowy Instytut Fryderyka Chopina/The Fryderyk Chopin Institue (NIFC). *Internet Chopin Information Center*. Accessed August 5, 2017 www.en.chopin.nifc.pl/chopin/main/page

Niecks, Frederick. *Chopin, as a Man and Musician*, 3rd ed. Reprint 1902.

Opieński, Henryk, ed. *Chopin's Letters*. Trans. Ethel Lilian Voynich. New York: Knopf, 1931. Reprint, New York: Dover, 1988.

Rink, John and Jim Samson, eds. *Chopin Studies II*. Cambridge and New York: Cambridge University Press, 1994.

Rosen, Charles. *The Romantic Generation*. Cambridge, Mass.: Harvard University Press, 1995.

Samson, Jim, ed. *The Cambridge Companion to Chopin*. Cambridge and New York: Cambridge University Press, 1992.

Samson, Jim. *Chopin*. New York: Schirmer, 1997.

Samson, Jim, ed. *Chopin Studies*. Cambridge and New York: Cambridge University Press, 1988.

Samson, Jim. *The Music of Chopin*. Oxford: Clarendon Press; New York: Oxford University Press, 1994.

Sand, George. *Lucrezia Floriani*, trans. Julius Eker. Chicago: Academy Chicago Publishers, 1993.

Sand, George. *Winter in Majorca*, trans. Robert Graves. Chicago: Academy Chicago Publishers, 1978.

Schenker, Heinrich. *Five Graphic Music Analyses*. New York: Dover Publications, 1969.

Slonimsky, Nicolas. *Lexicon of Musical Invective*, 2nd ed. Seattle and London: University of Washington Press, 1965.

Smialek, William and Maja Trochimczyk, eds. *Frédéric Chopin: A Research and Information Guide*, 2nd ed. New York and London: Routledge, 2015.

Sowinski, Albert. *Les Musiciens polonaise et slaves*. Paris, 1857. Reprint, New York: Da Capo Press, 1971.

Szulc, Tad. *Chopin in Paris: The Life and Times of the Romantic Composer*. New York: Scribner, 1998.

Trochimczyk, Maja, ed. *After Chopin: Essays in Polish Music*. Los Angeles: Polish Music Center at USC, 2000.

Weiss, Pierro and Richard Taruskin, eds. *Music in the Western World: A History in Documents*, 2nd ed. Belmont, Cal.: Schirmer, 2008.

Załuski, Iwo and Pamela Załuski. *Chopin's Poland*. London: Peter Owen, 1996.

Suggested Reading

A number of books have been written about Chopin aimed at linking his character and circumstances with the emotive and introspective content of his music. The most prominent of writings from the composer's era is the book by Chopin's musical colleague and friend Franz Liszt, published in 1852. Liszt's account of Chopin is believed to have been written mostly by Princess Carolyne zu Sayn-Wittgenstein, who had a long relationship with the Hungarian composer. A more comprehensive study of Chopin's creative life was published by Frederick Niecks, *Frederick Chopin as a Man and Musician* (1902). This book especially informs on music and musical activities in Poland before and during Chopin's lifetime and discusses musical life in the various cities that relate to Chopin's biographical timeline. Niecks additionally provides insightful comments on Chopin's music. Early publications on Chopin and his music are easily downloadable from Internet sources.

Among more recent (second half of the 20th century) biographies is the work by Adam Zamoyski, *Chopin: A New Biography* (1980). Along with applying detailed information on Polish culture to Chopin's life, this book sorts through some of the myths that have been perpetuated about the composer. As with much of the literature on Chopin, reference to the composer's correspondence is central to the documentation. In his book *Chopin in Paris: The Life and Times of the Romantic Composer* (1998), Tad Szulc addresses the complexity of Chopin as a person, concentrating on his 18 years in Paris.

The collection of essays compiled by Halina Goldberg, *The Age of Chopin: Interdisciplinary Inquiries* (2004), explores the context of Chopin's achievements as a composer by considering Polish history, other art forms, and the ideals of Romanticism. Excerpts from the writings of Chopin's students provided the resource for Jean-Jacques Eigeldinger's *Chopin: Pianist and Teacher as Seen by His*

Pupils (2013). Comments that can be traced back to the composer by performers continuing his teaching tradition have influenced the interpretations of specific works.

The basic outline of Chopin and his artistic achievements, as highlighted in this volume, have served as the grounding for films and novels. Two elaborations of the relationship with George Sand are the film "Impromptu" (1991) and Leon Thornber's *Bitter Glory: A Novel of the Life of Chopin* (1939).

Readings can only augment the insight into the artistry of Frédéric Chopin that is to be gleaned from the composer's music. In *Simply Chopin*, I have focused on the most frequently performed and recorded musical works. A notable performance achievement is the 11-disc set of *The Chopin Collection*, recordings by Artur Rubinstein on RCA from 1946-1967. From this reference, comparison to performances by other celebrated pianists can illuminate subtleties of interpretation that have given Chopin's music prominence in concert programming. Myriad performances can be accessed through web-based resources such as YouTube and music streaming services.

About the Author

William Smialek is emeritus vice president and professor of music at Jarvis Christian College in Hawkins, Texas. He received his Ph.D. in musicology from the University of North Texas and was a Fulbright Scholar in Poland in 1979-80. His books include *Frédéric Chopin: A Research and Information Guide* (2015), *Ignacy Feliks Dobrzyński and Musical Life in Nineteenth-Century Poland* (1991), and *The Symphony in Poland* (1982). Dr. Smialek's scholarly work also includes a number of papers and reviews on nineteenth- and twentieth-century music and culture in Eastern Europe.

A Word from the Publisher

Thank you for reading *Simply Chopin*!

If you enjoyed reading it, we would be grateful if you could help others discover and enjoy it too.

Please review it with your favorite book provider such as Amazon, BN, Kobo, Apple Books, or Goodreads, among others.

Again, thank you for your support and we look forward to offering you more great reads.

www.ingramcontent.com/pod-product-compliance
Lightning Source LLC
Chambersburg PA
CBHW030200100526
44592CB00009B/365